Regional Planning for
Health Care System in Jammu and Kashmir

About the Author

Rais Akhtar, formerly Professor & Head, Department of Geography, and Dean, Faculty of Social Sciences, University of Kashmir, is currently National Fellow, Centre for the Study of Regional Development, Jawaharlal Nehru University, New Delhi. He was a Full member of the International Geographical Union Commission on Environment, Health and Development (1988-2000). He has been awarded a number of international fellowships, including Leverhulme Overseas Visiting Fellow (University of Liverpool), Henry Chapman Fellow (University of London), and Visiting Fellow (University of Sussex). He has to his credit a number of research papers published in national and international journals of repute. He is the author/editor of eleven books. During 1988-99, he was Member of the Working Group on Health and Population and Communicable Diseases of Indian Planning Commission, Ministry of Health and Family Welfare, New Delhi.

Rais Akhtar was one of the lead Authors on the chapter Human Health of United Nations Intergovernmental Panel on Climate Change (IPCC) (1999-2007), which is the joint winner of Nobel Peace prize for 2007.

Regional Planning for Health Care System in Jammu and Kashmir

Rais Akhtar
National Fellow
Center for the Study of Regional Development
Jawaharlal Nehru University, New Delhi 110067

CONCEPT PUBLISHING COMPANY, NEW DELHI-110059

ISBN-13: 978-81-8069-627-5 **ISBN-10: 81-8069-627-8**

First Published 2009

Published and Printed by

Concept
Since 1974

Concept Publishing Company
Regd. Office:
A/15-16, Commercial Block, Mohan Garden
New Delhi-110059 (India)
Phones : 25351460, 25351794, *Fax* : 091-11-25357109
Email : publishing@conceptpub.com,
website: www.conceptpub.com

Editorial Office:
H-13, Bali Nagar, New Delhi-110 015, India.

Cataloging in Publication Data--*Courtesy:* D.K. Agencies (P) Ltd. <docinfo@dkagencies.com>

Akhtar, **Rais,** 1946-
Regional planning for health care system in Jammu and Kashmir / Rais Akhtar.
p. cm.
Includes bibliographical references.
Includes index.
ISBN 13: 9788180696275 ISBN 10: 8180696278

1. Health facilities--India--Jammu and Kashmir--Regional disparities. 2. Health planning--India--Jammu and Kashmir. 3. Regional medical programs--India--Jammu and Kashmir. I. Title.

DDC 362.10954 22

Preface

Who gets "what, where and why" is a popular catch phrase. It is used with the Inverse Care Law by social scientists while pondering over the problem of unequal distribution of social welfare care in western countries. How widespread are such disparities–globally and, especially, in the third world countries? Vast majorities of people in the third world suffer from high mortality and morbidity. In contrast, the affluent enjoy a health status comparable to that of most people in developed countries. The distribution of health services are also skewed, resources are directed at sophisticated facilities in towns while the rural majority remains practically unserved. From the health care perspective the noble World Health Organization (WHO) goal of "Health for All by 2000" has been a great driver for Third World countries, which are committed to achieving the equity in the provision of health care. Though the WHO objective could not be achieved but it helped encourage health planners to minimize the gaps in the provision of health care facilities.

In the last fifty years, a lot of progress has taken place in Jammu and Kashmir. Total number of Medical Institutions in the State increased from 124 in 1950-51 to 905 in 1970-71 and 3692 in 2000-01. Percentage increase during 1950-51 and 2000-01 is 2877.

Population-Medical Institution ratio is an important indicator of progress on health care delivery pattern. In 1950-51, 26242 persons were dependent on one medical institution with the increase in the number of medical institutions; the Population-Medical Institution ratio was reduced to 3290 in 1980-81 and 2727 in 2000-01. Bed strength in hospital and dispensary is another important indicator of health care development. In 1950-51, there were 1472 beds which increased to 5422 in 1980-81 and 11481 in 2000-01. It is evident that the increase in the number of beds has not been substantial, as a number of dispensaries were established without inpatient bed provision. Bed-population ratio which was 2292 in 1950-51 declined to 1102 in 1980-81 and 877 in 2000-01. It appears that there has been an overall development in the provision of health care facilities in the State of Jammu and Kashmir. However, when data are analysed spatially inequalities clearly emerged in its distribution pattern. Thus regional health care plan must be based on concrete demographic, social, cultural, and economic conditions prevailing in the region.

New Delhi **Rais Akhtar**

Acknowledgement

I am grateful to the Indian Council of Social Science Research for sanctioning the project entitled: *Spatial Issues in the Planning of a Health Care System in J & K (1 -74/95/RP).* The submission of the project report was delayed due to various unavoidable reasons, including the disturbed conditions in J & K. Completion of the project was further delayed because of non-availability of 2001 Census data, provisional tables of which were published only in the middle of 2005.

I am thankful to Dr. G.M. Rather for his research assistance, Dr. Harmeet Singh for his assistance in the preparation of maps and Mr. M.A. Tak for conducting field work. I am indebted to my wife Nilofar and daughter Shirin, for their cooperation and assistance.

I hope that the project report will be a sound foundation for the future health care development in the State of Jammu and Kashmir.

Rais Akhtar

Contents

List of Figures

1

Physiographic Set-up of Jammu and Kashmir

The State of Jammu and Kashmir comprising the Divisions of Jammu, Kashmir and Ladakh has an area of 2.22 lakh sq.km. According to the Census of 1981, its population was about 5.95 million that increased to 10.07 million in 2001. It is bounded by Tibet in the east, China and Afghanistan in the north and Pakistan in the west, while the southern and south-eastern boundaries are formed by the States of Punjab and Himachal Pradesh of the country. Morphologically, the State is divided into three distinct regions *i.e.* Jammu, Kashmir and Ladakh and each of these regions has distinct physiographic features.

JAMMU REGION

(i) The Outer Plains

Southern portion of the State, is rimmed by an alluvial plain formed by Chenab, Tawi and Ravi rivers and their tributaries. In width it varies from seven to thirty kilometres. This plain region constitutes a part of the Great Plains of Northern India. It is a contiguous region with the plains of Punjab in the south. The altitude varies between 325 to 350 metres in the outer plain areas. Akhnoor, Ranbirsinghpura (R.S. Pura), Samba and Kathua towns fall in this region.

(ii) The Siwaliks

To the north of the Jammu Plains, for distance of about 200 km between Ravi and Jhelum rivers, lie the youngest mountains of the sub-continent *i.e.* the Siwaliks. The width of Siwaliks is between 20 to 50 km. and height between 600 to 1220 metres above sea lèvel (Hussain, 1994). The lowly Siwalik hills constitute the Outer Himalayan zone on the northern periphery of the Indo-Gangetic plain, forming a series of foothills with an average height of 1,000 metres only (Raza *et al.*, p. 4).

These young tertiary hills known as Siwaliks form a wall separating the Middle Himalayas from the outer plains of which they form a part geomorphologically but not geologically as these are classed with the plains. (Raina, 1971, p.24).

The western region of the Siwaliks has a wide expanse with massive conglomerates, boulders and clay. Economically unimportant, the western region of the Outer Hills is vast and varied. The population is distributed in small scattered settlements throughout this belt.

(iii) The Middle Himalayas

The Middle Himalayas are spread in numerous ranges rising as high as 3657 to 4572 metres above sea level. More or less converging ranges are intersected by deep gorges through which rivers flow. These rivers are fed with snow from the mountains. These alluvial tracts look like longitudinal valleys, as in Bhaderwah, whose physiographically and climate make it resemble Kashmir. Hence the valley of Bhadarwah is called CHHOTA KASHMIR (lesser Kashmir). The longitudinal valley of Banihal though very narrow is to the north of the Pir Panjal and has similar morphological features of a typical Middle Mountain character. Perceptual snows on the higher elevations of the mountains which rise above 4572 m including the Brahma Peak, which rises above 6400 m form a typical feature.

The economic importance of this physical division is at premium with exploitation of its forest resources and prospects of mineral wealth. As a source of hydro-electric power, this region has a sufficient potential.

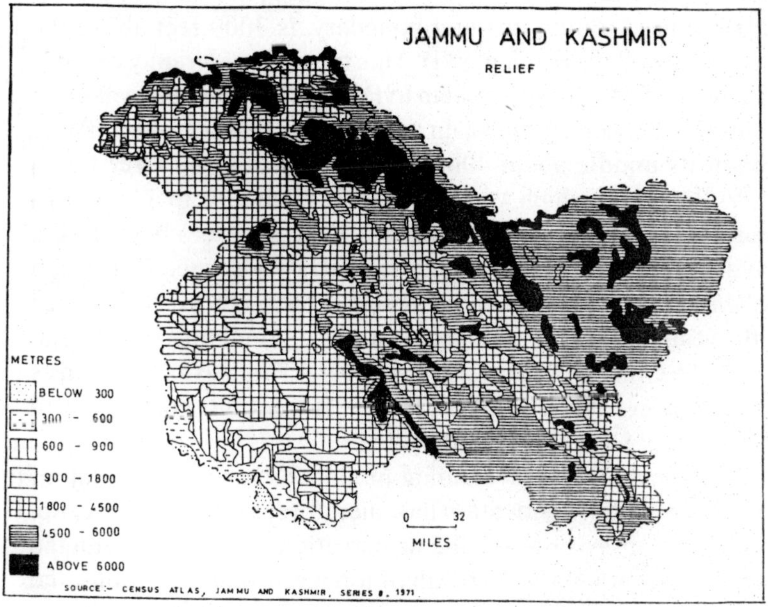

Figure 1.1: Jammu and Kashmir Relief

Beyond the Pir Panjal after crossing the Jawahar Tunnel at 2194.56 m above sea level, the beautiful valley of Kashmir is open to view. Enclosed by high mountain chains in all sides except for certain passes and a narrow gorge at Baramulla, the valley is the drainage basin of the river Jhelum and its tributaries. This valley *dun,* tectonic in origin, is like other sub-Himalayan *duns.* (Raina, 1971, pp. 26-27).

The Valley of Kashmir

The valley of Kashmir lies in between the Greater Himalaya and Pir Panjal, consisting of the districts of Anantnag, Pulwama, Baramulla, Srinagar, Budgam, and Kupwara. The valley of Kashmir has an area of 15,853 sq km. More than 259 sq km area in the valley is under water. The general elevation of the valley is about 1828 m above sea level. According to Koul, the lowest point in the valley has an elevation of 5,200 feet, and the mean elevation is 6,000 feet above sea level. The lowest pass (Banihal) in the Pir Panjal range, forming its outer boundary, is 3000 feet above the level of the valley (Koul, p. xxi). This type of topography extends over about 180 km from Shopian to Baramulla. The open valley of Kashmir is formed by the basin of the upper Jhelum, which flows through its middle about 40km. Below Srinagar the river forms the Wullar Lake which varies in extent from 130 to 155 sq km according to the season. Its outlet is near Sopore, about 23 km above Baramulla, below which it enters its gorge. North and northeast of the valley is a broad mountain tract, eroded and drained north-westward by the Kishanganga and culminating in the axial zone of the Greater Himalayas. The Greater Himalayas themselves in Kashmir are less rugged and carry fewer high peaks than in neighbouring Uttarakhand and Nepal.

The slope of the surrounding mountains round the valley of Kashmir is gentle. Cultivation has, therefore, extended higher up, enabling an observer to see the demarcation contour between the plain and the mountain. As result of topographical conditions, the settlements have also spread in lower and higher elevations depending on the availability of water and nutrient rich soil needed for cultivation.

The valley of Kashmir narrows itself towards the north with the massive structure of the Kaji Nag range.

The Ladakh Region

Ladakh is one of the most elevated regions of the World. Its natural features may be explained by reference to two local terms: *changthang*, "northern" or "high plain", where the amount of level ground is considerable; and *rong*, "deep valley", where the contrary conditions prevail. The high plain predominates in the east, diminishing gradually westward. In the southeast of Ladakh lies Rupshu, a region of great brackish lakes and with a uniform height of above 13,500 ft. Cultivation there is difficult but a little beardless barley is raised; the small population consists mainly of nomadic shepherds. To the northwest of Rupshu, Zanskar is drained by Zanskar river which, flowing northward, joins the Indus below Leh. Zanskar is a bleak, inaccessible region where the people and the cattle remain indoors for half of the year. Cultivation by means of maturing and irrigation ranges from 9000 to 15000 ft. The people are divided into shepherds and those who follow pastoral pursuits on the upland valleys too high for cultivation and the Ladakhis who till the land around the valley villages. (Encyclopedia Britannica 1992)

The Greater Himalayas or the innermost line of the high ranges rises above the limits of perpetual snow with an average height extending to 3,048 m with peaks like Nanga Parbat (8,107 m). The central Himalayan axis bifurcates near Kullu with its northwesterly branch known as the Zanskar Range reaches the two peaks of Nun Kun (7,055 m). Some of the important passes in the Greater Himalayas and the Karakoram mountains include: Pir Panjal (3,494 m), Zoji La (3,529 m), Chilung La (4,401 m), Sarsank (5.716 m), and Singo La (5,097 m). (Raina, 1971). Beyond the great range, the subsidiary Zanskar and Ladakh ranges separate it from the trough of the Indus and its tributary Shyok. These rivers have their distant sources on the desolate plateaus of western Tibet and traverse Ladakh.

To sum up, it is evident from the physiographic description of the State of Jammu & Kashmir, that the task of health care planning in the three regions is daunting. Physical inaccessibility to health care centres is a major problem for achieving HEALTH CARE FOR ALL. Attempt has been made in the book to develop various models to be adopted in such heterogeneous region.

REFERENCES

Encyclopedia Britannica, Jammu & Kashmir, Chicago.1992, p. 587 and pp. 867-870.

Koul, Pandit Anand (undated). *Geography of Jammu & Kashmir State,* Light and Life Publishers, New Delhi.

Raina, A.N. (1971). *Geography of Jammu & Kashmir,* National Book Trust, New Delhi.

Raza, M. Ahmad A. and Mohammad, A. (1978). *The Valley of Kashmir: A Geographical Interpretation.* Vikas Publishing House Pvt. Ltd., New Delhi.

2

Physical and Socio-Economic Framework of Jammu and Kashmir

As said earlier Jammu and Kashmir State comprises mainly of mountainous regions with a small belt of plain area in the southern part of Jammu region. The main part of the State consists of the western section of Himalayas which besides containing many lofty mountain ranges varying from an elevation of 3000-6000 meters and above, also includes a number of side valleys, lakes, glaciers, plateaus and plain. The Pir Panjal range separates the Kashmir region from Jammu region in the South and Zanskar range separates Kashmir division from Ladakh division in the north. Analysis of the Table 2.1 reveals that there is a considerable variation in almost all physical and social economic indicators in the three divisions of Jammu and Kashmir.

In Jammu and Kashmir State, ethnic and religious barriers to medical care do not exist and on account of availability of free medical care at all the levels, even the poorest of the poor have access to public medical care. However physical barriers do exist and mould almost all health indicators in the three natural regions which lead to variation of health indicators and levels of health care facilities. In general most health care facilities are located in the urban areas of highest hierarchy. However, inaccessible remote mountainous areas lack health care facilities (Table 2.2).

Table 2.1: Physical and Socio-Economic Indicators in Three Natural Regions

Jammu and Kashmir from Health Perspective

Name of Natural Region/Division	*Average Altitude above mean sea level*	*Area (Sq. km)*	*Average Rainfall*	*Distribution of Population (%)*	*Density of Population*	*Density of Household*	*Settlement Density*	*Mean Max, Temperature*	*Mean Min. Temperature*
Jammu	970	21%	96.34	45	103.38	17.12	0.23	29.39	17.19
Kashmir	1586	19%	84.7	54	196.58	28.94	0.48	17.27	7.29
Ladakh	4500	69%	3.15	1.5%	1.39	6.27	0.02	12.27	-4.24

Table 2.2: Health Indicators in Three Natural Regions of J & K State

Natural Regions	*Medical Institutions*	*Density of Medical Institutions per sq. km*	*Density of Hospital Beds per sq. km*	*Density of Doctors per sq. km*	*Population per Medical Institution*
Jammu	2055	0.64	0.05	0.02	
Kashmir	1561	0.08	0.09	0.04	
Ladakh	13.20	0.0003	0.0004	0.00009	728

Demographic Structure

Demographic structure of the study area focuses on the distribution of population, age, sex structure, occupational structure, level of education and level of income.

Population Distribution

The total population of sample households in the sample villages was 2475 (Table 2.3). The highest population of sample household was in the village Tailbal (320), followed by Dalgate (263), and Chushoot (244). However the lowest population of sample household was found in the sample village of Rainawari (195), Sakti (150) and Manigam (158).

Table 2.3: Sample Villages

Region	Sample Village	Area In Hectares	Population 1981	Total Households	Households* Surveyed
Jammu	Sohal				20
	Kheri				20
	Purmandal				20
	Bera				20
	Purbhoo				20
Kashmir	Rainawari				20
	Manigam	606	3618		20
	Tailbal		2082		20
	Dalgate		1165	149	20
	Shalbugh		739	93	20
	Khonmoh	1973.27	5067	694	20
Ladakh	Thiksay				20
	Chushoot				20
	Sakti				20
	Nimu				20
J and K State Total					

Note: * Household is defined as a group of persons who commonly live together and would take meals from a common kitchen.

Age and Sex Structure

Analysis of the table 2.4 reveals that out of the total population of sample household, 55.54% were male and the remaining were female. Out of the total male population 31.75% were adults and the remaining were children belonging the age group of 0-7 years. Out of the total female population 26.01% were adults and the remaining 16.83% belong to the 0-7 age group.

Occupational Structure

It is evident from the table 2.5 that out of the total population of sample household 29.75 per cent are engaged in primary occupation, 30.33 per cent were practising secondary occupation and 27.92 per cent were engaged in tertiary occupation. The percentage of households having primary level of occupation was highest in the sample village of Sakti (53.3%), followed by Thiksay

(43.3%) and Tailbal (37%). However the population of sample households having primary level of occupation was lower in the sample of Rainawari (37%), Dalgate (20%), Shalbugh (20%) and Khonmoh (50%). (Table 2.5)

Table 2.4: Age and Sex Structure of Sample Villages (1999)

Sample Village/Region	*Male (% of Households Population)*		*Female (% of Households Population)*	
	Adult	*Children*	*Adult*	*Children*
Sohal	39.45	16.20	35.20	9.15
Kheri	32.09	20.14	32.84	14.93
Purmandal	33.55	22.98	28.57	14.9
Beru	37.51	18.03	35.24	9.02
Purkhoo	38.84	22.33	25.24	13.59
Jammu Region	36.28	20.06	31.41	12.32
Rainawari	40	12.9	37.9	9.21
Manigam	32	19	32.	17
Tailbal	35	20	25	20
Dalgate	39	18	29	14
Shalbugh	28	23	25	24
Khonmoh	34	21	28	17
Kashmir Region	34.66	18.98	24.48	16.87
Sakti	22	29.4	22.6	26
Chushoot	30.3	28.4	23.3	18.2
Thiksay	23.5	35.9	21.4	19.2
Nimu	21.5	35.6	21.3	21.8
Ladakh Region	24.32	32.32	22.15	21.3
J & K State Total	31.75	23.79	26.01	16.83

Source: Field Survey.

Highest population of sample household in secondary occupation was found in villages Purkhoo (70%), Beru (65%), Sohal (60%), Kheri (60%), Manigam (57%) and Rainawari (23%) followed by Tailbal (20%), Khonmoh (17%) Sakti (16.7).

However lowest percentage was found in the villages of Thiksay (6.7%) and Chushoat (10%) However, population and sample household involved in tertiary activities was highest in

Rainawari followed by Chushoot (56%), Thiksay (50%), Nimu (50%) and Tailbal (43%). However, the per cent of population of sample households involved in tertiary activities was lowest in Khonmoh (7%) (Table 2.5).

Table 2.5: Occupational Structure of Sample Villages (1999)

Sample	*Household in Different Categories of Occupation (% to total)*			
Village/Region	*Primary*	*Secondary*	*Tertiary*	*Others*
Sohal	20	60	20	—
Kheri	30	60	10	—
Purmandal	10	35	45	10
Beru	15	65	15	5
Purkhoo	X	70	20	10
Jammu Region	*15*	*58*	22	5
Rainawari	3.7	23	73.3	—
Manigam	30	57	—	13
Tailbal	37	20	43	—
Dalgate	20	—	—	80
Shalbugh	20	13	—	67
Khonmoh	50	17	7	26
Kashmir Region	26.78	21.66	20.56	31.00
Sakti	53.3	16.7	30	—
Chushoot	34	10	56	—
Thiksay	43.3	6.7	50	—
Nimu	36.7	13.3	50	—
Ladakh Region	*47.46*	*11.34*	*41.2*	—
J and K State Total	29.75	30.33	27.92	12

Source: Field Survey.

Levels of Education

Analysis of table 2.6 reveals that literacy rate of population of all sample households was 52.44 per cent. Some 23.15 per cent of households were having middle level of education, 28 per cent were having 9th level to level graduate education and 1.29 per cent were having above graduate level of education. However 47.56 per cent of total population sample households were illiterate.

Analysis of the table clearly shows that the percentage of population of sample villages having middle level of education was highest in the village Sakti (40%) followed by Dalgate (37%), Shalbugh (37%) and Manigam (23%). However lowest percentage was obtained for Dalgate (13%) and Thiksay (13.3%).

Table 2.6: Levels of Education in Sample Villages (1999)

Sample Village/Region	*No. of Households in Different Levels of Education (% to total)*			
	Upto 8th	*9th to Graduate*	*Above Graduate*	*Illiterate*
Sohal	55	30	X	15
Kheri	10	55	X	35
Purmandal	45	50	X	5
Beru	35	35	X	30
Purkhoo	20	30	X	50
Jammu Region	*33.00*	*40.00*	*X*	*27.00*
Rainawari	6.7	30	3.3	60
Manigam	23	37	10	30
Tailbal	3	30	—	67
Dalgate	37	13	—	60
Shalbugh	37	26	—	37
Khonmoh	20	20	10	40
Kashmir Region	21.12	26.00	3.88	49.00
Sakti	40	16.7	—	43.
Chushoot	6.7	30.0	—	63.3
Thiksay	16.7	13.3	—	70.0
Nimu	13.3	20.0	—	66.7
Ladakh Region	*15.34*	*18.00*	—	*66.66*
J and K State Total	*23.15*	*28.00*	*1.29*	*47.56*

Source: Field Survey.

Population with graduate level of education was noted in three villages *i.e.* Manigam (10%), Khonmoh (10%) and Rainawari (3.3%). The illiterate population was highest in the village Thiksay (70%) and Nimu (66.7%). However the lowest illiterate rate was found in the village Manigam (30%) followed by Shalbugh (37%) and Khonmoh (40%).

Monthly Income of Sample Households

A considerable variation in monthly income in different households have been noted in different sample villages (Table 2.7). Most of the households fall in the income level of Rs. 1600-3000. However the number of households having the income of above Rs. 6000 per month in the Jammu region is low.

The percentage of households in the income level of Rs. 500-1500 per month was high in the village Sakti (43.3%) followed by Tailbal (43%). Number of households in this income level was very low in village Manigam (7%), followed by Shalbugh (20%), Dalgate and Khonmoh (27% each).

Table 2.7: Monthly Income of Sample Villages (1999)

Sample Village/Region	*No. of Households in Different Levels of Income (% to total)*			
	Rs. 500-1500	*Rs. 1600-3000*	*Rs. 3000-6000*	*Above 6000*
Sohal	45	25	30	X
Kheri	45	40	10	5
Purmandal	75	25	—	—
Beru	45	45	10	—
Purbhoo	50	30	10	10
Jammu Region	52	33	12	3
Rainawari	27	20	16.4	36.6
Manigam	7	30	30	33
Tailbal	43	30	17	10
Dalgate	27	40	6	27
Shalbugh	20	37	37	6
Khonmoh	27	50	20	3
Kashmir Region	*25.17*	*34.50*	*21.06*	*19.27*
Sakti	43.3	30	20	6.7
Chusboot	23.3	23.4	23.3	30
Thiksay	16.7	40	30	13.3
Nimu	6.7	56.4	30	6.9
Ladakh Region	*26.00*	*37.96*	*23.34*	*12.70*
J & K State Total	34.39	35.16	18.80	11.65

Source: Field Survey.

The number of households in the income level of Rs 1600-3000 was high in the village Nimu (56.4%), Khonmoh (50%) and Dalgate (40%) and below 40 per cent in the remaining villages. The percentage of households in the income category of Rs 3000-6000 per month was lower than 40 per cent in all the sample villages and the same situation occured in all the sample villages regarding the income level of Rs. 6000 per month.

Population and Mortality Pattern

Distribution of Population

Population distribution in the state of J and K is highly uneven. Varied physical features result in the variation of population density. Figure 2.1 reveals the distribution of population density in district as per cent to total population of the State. It is evident from the figure that the Jammu region and the Kashmir region share the major chunk of the population. Ladakh, owing to its topographic features remains one of the lowest populated regions in the country.

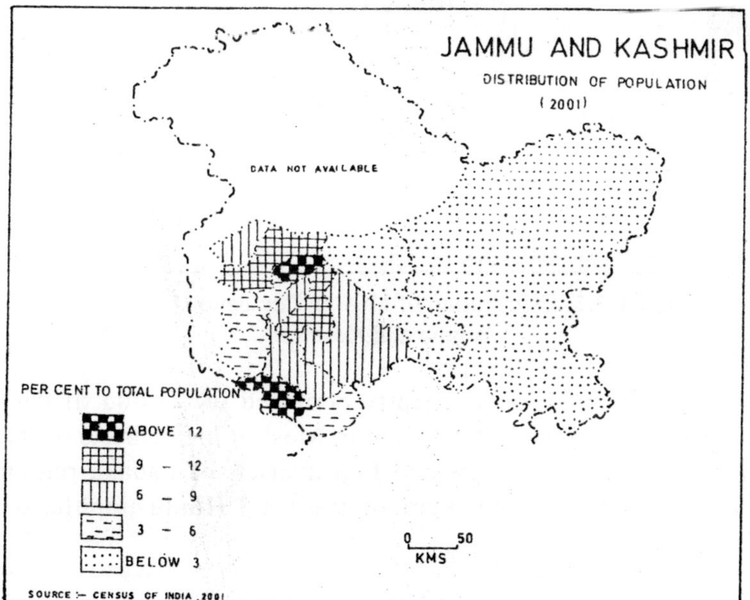

Figure 2.1: Distribution of Population (2001) in Jammu and Kashmir.

Distribution of Muslim/Hindu Population

Figure 2.2 reveals that Muslim population is mainly confined to the valley of Kashmir followed by Punch district in the Jammu region and Kargil in Ladakh region. Less than 10 per cent of the total Muslim population is confined in Kathua district. Some 10 to 30 per cent of Muslim population inhabit in Jammu and Ladakh districts.

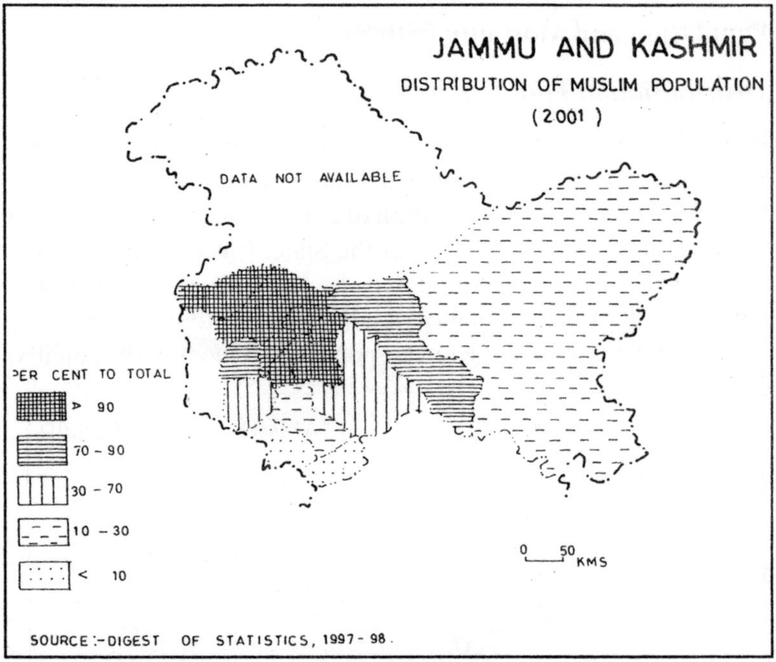

Figure 2.2: Distribution of Muslim Population (2001) in Jammu and Kashmir

Hindu population is mainly confined in Kathua district followed by Jammu and Udhampur. Most of the districts of the valley of Kashmir, Kargil and Leh districts of Ladakh region contain less than 5 per cent of the total Hindu population (Fig. 2.3).

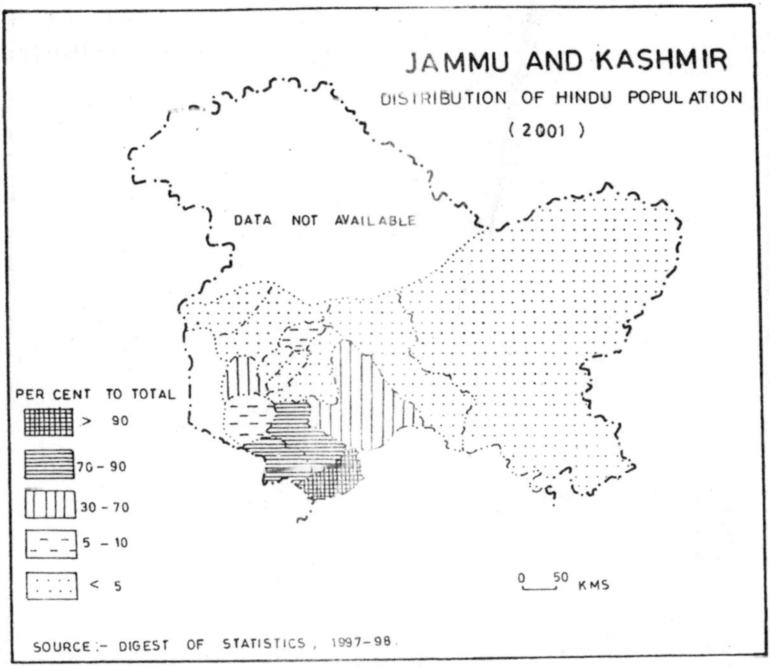

Figure 2.3: Distribution of Hindu Population (2001) in Jammu and Kashmir

Deaths Registered

Figure 2.4 depicts the spatial pattern of deaths registered in different districts.

Jammu district has the highest percentage of total deaths (more than 25%) and Leh and Kargil districts show the lowest percentage *i.e.* less than 2 per cent of the total deaths. Districts in the Kashmir valley fall between 2 and 10 per cent of total deaths.

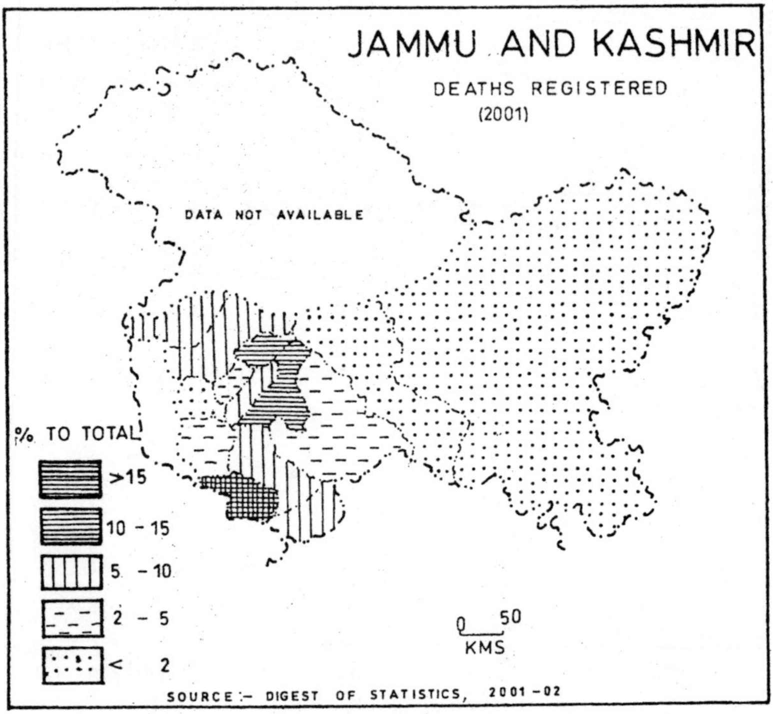

Figure 2.4: Death Registered (2001) in Jammu and Kashmir

3

Geography of Health Care Development in Mountainous Areas

The dispersed character of settlements, the small size of villages and urban centres and poor network of communication and transportation in mountainous areas, particularly in the State of Jammu and Kashmir, poses serious problems in the provision of services, including health care facilities. On the one hand, small population size of mountain settlements rules out the provision of basic services such as health care facilities in each and every village; on the other hand, the absence of suitable road network and transport services prevents the mountain population from utilizing basic health facilities in central places.

The low number of health facilities is considered one of the reasons for growing out-migration from mountainous areas such as Uttarakhand mountain region, and in some cases, for their complete depopulation. In this connection a comprehensive assessment of the geographical aspects of services in mountainous areas is a prerequisite in health care planning of mountainous areas. From the point of view of services including health care, mountainous areas are distinguished by the following:

(a) The poor accessibility of many populated places and the poor development of transportation/communication network;

(b) The dispersion of places over a large territory, and the small size of most of them (Ladakh is a good example);
(c) A sparse network of underdeveloped towns and a low level of urbanization in general and the presence of a primate city with high percentage of urban population to total population (Valley of Kashmir is a good example);
(d) The presence of seasonally inhabited places with significant seasonal fluctuations in population size and differences in the types of required services (Gujjar and Bakharwal transhumance in Jammu and Kashmir is a relevant example);
(e) A low level of intensity of agriculture and of marketable production (Ladakh region);
(f) A low level of industrial development and almost total absence of industrial labour techniques (both the Valley of Kashmir and Ladakh regions);
(g) The survival of a subsistence economy and of backward traditions in daily life. (Most of the Ladakh region and some parts of Valley of Kashmir and Jammu region.); and
(h) Presence of different socio and cultural groups, with varied health care seeking behaviour (Amchi system of medicine in Ladakh, Ayurveda in Jammu region, and Unani in the Valley of Kashmir).

The relationship between these geographical characteristics, on the one hand, and the level and type of health services on the other, affect the choice of types of service establishment and their spatial distribution.

The above mentioned peculiarities tend to hamper the development of the health sector, raise the costs of construction of establishments as well as operating costs, and greatly limit the accessibility of some types of services. The level of health care services achieved in mountainous areas will depend to a large extent on the general level of economic development; some peculiarities of the services rendered are caused by the character and distribution pattern of mountain settlements.

The availability of particular health care services plays a key role in shaping the living conditions of the population. The range of health care services in mountainous areas needs to be expanded, based on holistic health care planning, if living conditions in various natural regions of Jammu and Kashmir are to be improved and inequalities in health care provisions minimized.

The subsistence type of economy in most rural areas, particularly in Ladakh region; lack of resources for industrial development, and sparsely distributed settlements in Ladakh region have been of great hindrance in the development of services including health care provision. There is a growing need for redistribution of population and reconstruction of settlement patterns particularly in Ladakh region. Only an integrated approach to the problem of mountain development will yield the desired result of an improvement of consumer services. Therefore, an investigation of the assessment of services required by the people should involve geographers, economists, and sociologists.

Physical and socio-economic and cultural conditions vary in different mountainous areas, understanding of these variation is important for the development of services. More than 90 per cent of the State of Jammu and Kashmir is mountainous. The greater the relief and associated dispersion of population, the greater are the problems of providing health care services. Physiographically the region comprises (southwest to northeast) of the fertile Jammu and Punch plains (1000 to 2000 ft.) with satisfactory network of transportation and communications, the thickly forested (coniferous) Himalayan region (2000 to 7000 ft.) and heavily glaciated Pir Panjal Range with both sparse population and poor transportation network. The Valley of Kashmir at an elevation of 5300 ft, with good network of transportation and communication. The complex Central Himalayan ranges (more than 2000 ft), the upper Indus Valley (11000ft) and the Karakoram Range which contains K2 (28250 ft) the second highest peak in the world after Mt. Everest. The climate varies from alpine in the north-east to sub-tropical in the southwest. The mean temperature in January varies from 14° C at Jammu to –17° at Dras. Correspondingly, June temperatures are 33° C and 18° C. The State of Jammu and Kashmir contains about 1 per cent of the population of India (2001 Census). From the point of view of the rendering of health care services, three basic natural-geographical regions in Jammu and Kashmir may be distinguished. (Table 3.1)

1. *Jammu Region*: The region comprises the productive plains and the Lesser Himalayas. The Lesser Himalayas are composed of outer ranges, their wooded spurs and foothills, bordering a narrow piedmont strip, rarely 16 km. wide. The population density per sq. km. ranges as low as 59 in Doda and 508 in Jammu districts. Similarly, road length per lakh of population varies from 59 km in Poonch to 146 km in Kathua districts.
2. *The Valley of Kashmir*: The Valley of Kashmir is a deep asymmetrical basin lying between Pir Panjal and the western end of the Great Himalayan ranges at an average altitude of 5,300 feet. The region possesses good network of transportation and communication. Road length per lakh of population varies from 114 in Anantnag and as high as 177 in Badgam districts. The population density per sq km varies from 254 in Baramulla and 531 in Srinagar district.
3. *Ladakh Region*: Geologically complex and topographically immensely varied, the Ladakh region contains ranges reaching more than 20,000 feet in altitude and deeply entrenched, remote valleys. The city of Leh stands on a fan, 1,500 feet above sea level, with climate characterized by almost lack of rainfall, intense insolation (exposure to the sun's rays), and great diurnal and annual ranges of temperature. Life depends on melted water from the surrounding mountains. As a result of difficult topography, the population density per sq km greatly varies from 3 in Leh and 8 in Kargil districts. The road length per sq km is as low as 3 in Leh and 5 in Kargil. However, since the total population is low and is mainly confined to certain pockets, the figures for road length

per lakh of population looks higher 587 kms for Kargil and 989 kms for Leh districts. Each of these regions is further differentiated internally in terms of services depending on the infrastructural facilities, especially the road network. One of the distinctive features of the health sector and for that matter other services in the mountain region is the incomplete development of hierarchical system of services, particularly those services that are utilized on a daily basis, say for example dispensary and primary health services. For example, many mountain settlements lack dispensary facility. The poor development of transportation and mountainous topography in turn, hampers the use of medical institutions at higher hierarchical levels, such as sub-hospital and district hospital and specialised hospitals, such as S.N. Hospital in Leh District, Government Medical College Hospital and S.K. Institute of Medical Sciences, Srinagar District, and Government Medical College Hospital in Jammu District. Thus the usual operation of the health service sector is disrupted.

The norm of particular types of services in mountainous areas tend to be higher, as will be seen later in the chapter on Spatial Patterns of Health Care, than in other rural areas because of the dispersion of population and the poor accessibility of settlements. A rise in norms, in turn, leads to higher costs of services because of the increase in unit investment costs and in labour inputs. In this respect, mountainous areas resemble the underdeveloped regions of Ladakh and Doda districts of Jammu region. The provision of health services in the mountain regions is thus affected by purely economic reasons.

The impact of mountain settlement on the provision of services can be illustrated by the distribution of data on the developmental activities (Table 3.1). The three districts under study represent the three diverse regions–Srinagar for the Valley of Kashmir; Jammu for the Jammu region, and Leh for the Ladakh region. It is evident from the table that most of the indicators of development, *i.e.*

Table 3.1: Indicators of Development in the Three Regions (2001)

Districts	*Density of population (per sq. kms.)*	*Process of Urbanization (% of total population)*	*Percentage of villages electrified*	*Population per medical institution*	*Road length for 100 sq. kms of area*	*Road length per lakh of population*	*Students per lakh of population*	*Population coverage for school (1999)*	*Workers per 1000 persons*	*Cultivable areas as % of reported area*
SRINAGAR	531	78.59	100	4534	64	120	15502	1131	30.81	52.94
JAMMU	508	44.45	100	2944	57	112	21024	708	32.82	43.44
LEH	3	23.39	89.28	717	3	989	17711	340	50.14	22.22

Source: Based on Census Data and Govt. of Jammu and Kashmir: Indicators of Regional Development, 2000-2001, Directorate of Economics and Statistics.

population density, process of urbanization, electrification in rural areas, road length, students per lakh of population, and cultivable area are distributed in accordance with the topographical conditions and transport network. Since the population is low in comparison to the districts of Srinagar and of Jammu small number of people are dependent on one medical institution in Leh. Similar is the case with population coverage per school.

It is evident that health care planning of such a diverse region is difficult, and different solutions have to be found for different regions.

One of the most serious problems in mountainous areas is the poor accessibility of health care services. The dispersion of settlement creates significant problems in this regard. There are two ways of making basic services more accessible: one is to consolidate rural settlements; the other is to preserve the present settlement patterns, but to provide year-round transport services so that the villagers of any small village can use the health care service established in a central village. At the same time, all mountain dwellers should be provided with essential medicines from the nearby central health dispensary/primary health centre.

The introduction of a mobile medical van, visiting different villages if connected by road or through a drug men whose duty should be to visit each and every village in their respective areas. Such experiments have been very successful in mountainous areas in Vietnam.

Nonetheless the aim of health planning of such region as Ladakh should therefore be an optimal combination of the two approaches, i.e. both consolidation of small settlements and the development of transportation and communication.

The case of Jammu region and the Valley of Kashmir is different, and particularly in the plain and homogeneous areas the inequalities can be minimized with the help of location-allocation methods by providing extra health care facilities in deficit regions. This will be discussed in detail in subsequent chapters on spatial patterns of health care facilities in Jammu and Kashmir.

4

Health Care Patterns and Planning: Conceptual Framework

The provision of health care contributes significantly in minimizing the impact of the environment on malnutrition, parasite infested water, lack of sanitary facilities, inadequate housing and widespread ignorance, prevailing in the most developing regions including Jammu and Kashmir.

However, Maurice King rightly asserted that the cleavage of the world into rich nations and poor ones, divides care in sickness quite as sharply as it does any other aspect of the human condition. In this the great division of mankind, the rich have money and medical skills in comparative abundance, the poor have not. (King, 1966). These facts determine the nature of the entire practice of medicine in developing countries. Commenting on inequalities Prescott and Jamison in their study of health resource availability in China state, that despite egalitarian system in the distribution of hospitals there exist inequalities (Prescott and Jamison, 1985). In India too for instance the growth of hospitals was not in coterminus with the increase in population in eastern Rajasthan and western Madhya Pradesh. Instead high hospital availability areas were scattered all over the country. The low population density and a special preference to the north eastern region and Ladakh area of Jammu and Kashmir, resulted in the high availability of hospital facilities.

Commenting on the Rostowian model of development, Vincente Navarro, rejected the Rostowian determinants of under-development, and argued that under-development and the uneven distribution of resources inside and outside the health sector, is not due to:

(a) the absence of culture and technologic diffusion from developed to developing countries,
(b) the scarcity of capital in poor nations, or
(c) the presence of dual economies in under-developed countries. (Navarro, 1974)

Regarding the *first assumption* of cultural and technological diffusion, India possesses one of the best medical technologies as can be seen in Bombay, Delhi and other metropolitan areas. Both public and private sector possess sophisticated technology, though it does not mean that the imports of foreign technology is always good in the country's interest. Such cultural diffusion has been defined by Candau, the late Director General of the WHO, as "cultural imperialism". The scheme of importing used donated high technology medical equipments through the American Associations of Physician of Indian Origin (AAPIO) in association with the Medical Council of India may give an added fillip to acquire inappropriate and unnecessary technology. This will only push up the cost of medicine not only in private institutions, but in public hospitals as well. In a country where there are numerous cases of failing medical ethics which include inappropriate drug formulations—as reflected in the patterns of demand created by the doctor-patient nexus and unnecessary medical tests and surgery. The extent to which medicine is now viewed as a business is reflected in the rush of advertisements of diagnostic centres that have begun to sprout on the walls of the Metropolises and in trains and buses, as if the equipment were television sets or pressure cookers with the establishment of large number of modern hospitals in recent years, India is becoming an important destination for medical tourism for patients from the Middle East as well as from

European countries. Regarding the *second Rostowian assumption* or scarcity of resources, seems not very relevant. Apart from the importation of medical technology by both public and private sectors, tremendous progress took place in India since Independence, on the provision of health care facilities. Table 4.1 reveals that the number of doctors and beds has increased eight and six times and that of nurses by more than fifteen times.

Table 4.1: Achievements Since 1950

	Doctors	Hospitals	Beds	Nurses	Medical Colleges	Annual Output of Doctors
1950	65,000	133	1,25,000	18,500	30	959
1990	3,65,000	11,254	6,19,433	2,64,504	128	12,292
1998	5,03,900	15,188	6,65,639	6,07,376	165	13,170*

* For the year 1994

Source: Ministry of Health and Family Welfare, New Delhi, India Annual, New Delhi. *The Politics of Health in India,* R. Jeffery 1988, p. 245; and *Health Information of India,* 1997 & 1998 Ministry of Health and Family Welfare, New Delhi, 2000.

The number of medical colleges has gone up from 30 in 1950, 128 in 1990 to 165 in 1998. In rural areas, there were 2300 Primary Health Centres and 1,37,000 Sub-Centres as on 1990. These figures rose to 23,179 and 1,37,006 respectively in 1998.

Another interesting feature related to the migration of doctors from India is shown in table 4.2. Table 4.2 reveals that the majority of Indian doctors who went abroad for specialization belong to surgery and only an insignificant number *i.e.*, 45 belong to public health, which is so vital from the points of view of the Third World. This is a clear evidence that majority of the doctors don't want to serve their own country and the state, and wish to remain in western countries, United States and the United Kingdom, where the surgery and general medicine are more in demand than public health, T.B., Chest and Pathology, which are more relevant in Third World countries.

Table 4.2: Subject-Wise Distribution of Indian Doctors Trained Abroad Registered as on 31.12.1998

S. No.	*Subject*	*Total Number*	
		1990	*1998*
1.	Surgery	1601	1678
2.	General Medicine	1187	1216
3.	Obstetrics/Gynae	716	747
4.	Pediatrics	414	443
5.	Ophthalmology	297	306
6.	Anesthesiology	264	282
7.	Pathology	89	100
8.	Psychiatry	85	87
9.	Radiology	75	78
10.	Dentistry	65	66
11.	TB-Chest Diseases	51	51
12.	Medicine and Surgery	59	62
13.	Public Health	45	45
14.	Others	779	532

Source: Health Information of India, Ministry of Health and Family Welfare, New Delhi, 1991, p. 103; 1997 & 1998, p. 118.

In this context Anderson has rightly said that we look at the type of morbidity prevalent in surveyed population (i.e., infectious diseases and malnutrition) and at the comparative effectiveness of the different health activities for combating this morbidity, it would seem that environmental health services and preventive personnel health services should be given far higher priority than curative services, and particularly hospital services. Inspite of this, "the production of human resources, through the medical education imported from developed societies serves to perpetuate this hospital-oriented, curative medicine approach which only strengthens the mal-distribution of resources according to type of care by replicating the consumption of health resources prevalent in developed societies. (Anderson, 1973) The *third Rostowian assumption* dealing with the existence of dual economies and societies is reflected in the existence of an unequal distribution of health resources between the cities and the rural hinterlands, with western "hospital based" medicine in the cities and the indigenous and "less developed" form of medicine in the rural areas. According to Navarro "this dualism is considered to have come about, first, because of the lack of diffusion of Western, developed medicine to the rural areas, and second because of lack of resource and investment capital in those areas. (Navarro, 1974) These explanations pertaining to the existence of indigenous system of medicine show the lack of 'knowledge about the history of the origin of indigenous systems particularly the Ayurveda, Unani and Siddha Systems in the context of South Asia and Ayurveda, Unani and Amchi Medical Systems in Jammu and Kashmir. These systems grew over a period of thousands of years and much older then the western system. In fact the indigenous or traditional system of medicine that used to serve the vast majority of the population was greatly discouraged by Colonialists. However, inspite of attempts by the western system to eliminate other "irregular", systems or bring them into line, medical pluralism is typical of most societies. (Janzen, 1978) According to Bhardwaj the traditional medical system touches the vast majority of people. (Bhardwaj, 1980) A case study on Unani System of medicine in Aligarh town in northern India, conducted by Nilofar Izhar suggests that patients attend to Unani Clinic irrespective of socio-economic and cultural variations (Table 4.3) (Izhar, 1990).

It is obvious that medical pluralism is a resource and not hindrance in health care development.

Medical pluralism in Jammu and Kashmir has been studied in separate chapters on Health Care Behaviour in Jammu, Srinagar and Leh districts.

The above Rostowian assumptions failed to explain the health care under-development in India. Lack of planning and economic and political control of resources by specific interests and social groups lead to uneven distribution, type of health care, by region, by social class, and by sub-sectors (public/private) of human health resources (Navarro, 1974). A detailed account on the inequalities in health care facilities in Jammu and Kashmir will be discussed in subsequent chapters.

Table 4.3: The Practice of Medical Pluralism (Percent of sample patients opting for traditional Unani Medicine as their first choice and shifting to Unani Medicine from modern and other traditional systems, by type of illness).

Types of Illness	*Unani First Choice*	*Previous Other Treatment*	
		Modern	*Other*
Depression	11	69	20
Severe headache	12	84	04
Severe stomach pain	10	85	05
Urinary problems	49	42	09
Hypertension	—	100	—
Cough and Cold	88	12	—
Stomach Disorder	96	04	—

What countries in the Third World actually need is a model of health care in which both manpower and hospital/health centres are distributed in accordance with population distribution, with emphasis on rural, backward, tribal and mountainous and endemic areas. This might demand the introduction of spatial planning at micro-level in order to distribute facilities on the basis of equity.

One of the serious lapses in the health planning process is the lack of understanding of the organization of regional structure and where to adopt equity and efficiency models in the provisions of health facilities. Both equity (to minimize maximum distance) and efficiency (to minimize aggregate travel) considerations are adopted in the formulation of health care plans. The equity consideration aims at improving and bringing every settlement within a few kilometres of a health facility. The efficiency aspect concerns the utilization of existing manpower and facilities as efficiently as possible. It would be appropriate to study the socio-economic and physical framework of the region before emphasizing the application of these two criteria.

Equity criterion is ideal in the provision of amenities including health facilities. However, the basic premise before applying equity model is that the region where facilities are to be located, is a homogenous area. Particularly there is an efficient system of transport and communication network with not much variation, as well as there is homogeneity in the size and distribution of settlements. However, in a region such as Jammu and Kashmir with wide socio-economic and physical variations, no single model can be applied throughout the state. The pre-requisite for application of either model-equity or efficiency, is to demarcate the area into homogenous regions.

The adoption of method of locational analysis as mentioned under methodology may go a long way in increasing geographical accessibility to health centres, and thereby minimizing inequalities.

REFERENCES

Anderson, O.W. (1973). *Health Care: Can there be Equity?* John Wiley and Sons, New York. Quoted from Navarro, V., *Ibid*, p. 17.

Bhardwaj, S.M. (1980). Medical pluralism and homoeopathy: A geographic perspective, *Social Science and Medicine*, Vol. 14B, pp. 209-219.

Izhar, N., Patient origins and usage of a Unani Clinic in Aligarh town, India, *Social Science and Medicine*, Vol. 30, No. 10, 1990. p. 1140.

Janzen, J.M. (1978). The comparative study of medical systems as changing social system. *Social Science and Medicine*, Vol. 12, pp. 121-129.

King, M. (ed) (1966). *Medical Care in Developing Countries,* Oxford University Press.

Navarro, V. (1974). The under-development of health or the health of under-development; An analysis of the distribution of human health resources in Latin America, *International Journal of Health Services,* Vol. 4, No. 1, pp. 5-27.

Navarro, V., *op cit.*

Navarro. V., *op cit.*, p. 9.

Prescott, N. and Jamison, D.T. (1985). The distribution and impact of health resource availability in China, *International Journal of Health Planning and Management,* Vol. 1, No. 1, pp. 45-56.

5

Spatial Patterns of Health Care Facilities: Introduction and Methodological Scenario

Introduction

Inequality, in its various forms, is one of the most serious problems facing the contemporary world. Most of us are aware of the contrast between the 'haves' and 'have-nots' of our own society, and we also know something of differences in living standards among peoples elsewhere. There is widespread agreement that such gross inequalities as exist today are unjust, and that we should work towards a more equal world. But slums still survive, depressed regions remain so, and the 'development gap' between the rich and poor nations seems not to be narrowing significantly. How does inequality arise, why does it persist, and what can be done to reduce or eliminate it? (Smith, 1979)

"Who gets what, where and why" has been a popular catch-phrase, along with Inverse Care Law, used by social scientists in the course of discussing the unequal distribution of social welfare care in Western countries. How much more widespread are such disparities globally and in many parts of the Third World specifically? In the Third World the great majority of people suffer excess mortality and morbidity, while in contrast the affluent enjoy a health status similar to that of most people in developed countries. The health services also show a lopsided pattern with expenditure concentrated on sophisticated facilities in the towns, leaving the rural majority practically unserved. From the health care perspective the noble World Health Organisation (WHO) slogan "Health for All by 2000" has proven a great incentive to Third World countries, which are seriously concentrating on achieving equiatable distribution of health care facilities.

Primary Health Care

The current WHO approach on primary health care addresses some key issues related to this equality/inequality dimension, such as self-reliance, community participation, inter-sectoral collaboration, integration of primary health care often including traditional medicine with secondary and tertiary care and provision of services to vulnerable and under-served areas. Thus, in principle primary health care could be a useful instrument for coping with problems of inequality in health care. However, to translate this philosophy into reality is an uphill task, mainly owing to widespread intra-regional variations, meager health budgets, and the uniqueness of each country. R. Stock has starkly synthesized the plight of the Third World (Stock, 1985):

> "Seven years after the Alma-Ata Declaration, the persistent and deepening under-development of health in the Third World overshadows the scattered and limited evidence of progress. After a decade of global recession, the already impoverished and dependent nations of the Third World are confronted with massive and deepening crises. Huge international debts, in some cases amounting to 50 per cent or even 100 per cent of the gross national product, have necessitated the cancellation of development programmes as well as slashing of the recurrent expenditure necessary to maintain pre-existing services. Most national administrations remained unwilling to radically reallocate resources to ensure a socially-just

> distribution of health services; the quantitative and qualitative disparities in health care provision exposed a decade ago by Navarro persist almost everywhere in the Third World. The persistence of such disparities reflects the distribution of effective political and economic power, with ruling classes predictably protecting their own "national interests". Meanwhile the health consequences associated with Third World countries' food shortages, the export of health-threatening industries to the Third World, and the vigorous promotion of potentially lethal products such as pesticides, herbicides, infant formula and pharmaceuticals is increasing, thus creating additional pressures on the inadequate existing health care System". (Stock, 1985).

According to the Draft Document on Primary Health Care in India, "A district is normally covered by 8 to 12 primary health centres. The medical officer incharge of a primary health centre has the overall responsibility for providing integrated health services, namely curative, preventive and promotive to the population, of about 80,000 to 1,00,000. Each primary health centre has sub-centres which cater to a population of about 5,000. Each sub-centre, is manned by a male and female multi-propose health worker. They provide integrated package of services: medical care, maternal and child health care, family planning, control of malaria and other communicable diseases, environmental sanitation, collection of vital statistics and health education". (Working Group, 2000)

In view of the above it is vital that planning agencies must focus their attention to the spatial patterns for the provision of PHC's in different regions taking into account the population distribution. However, provision of health care must be based on the need and demand of the population. Health care behaviour studies should be carried out in different socio-economic and cultural regions in order to assess the preference for a particular system—allopathic or indigenous by the population. Lack of such health behaviour surveys leads to the paradox, "inspite of the availability of these facilities, their utilization is very meagre—hardly 10 to 20 per cent". (Griffith, 1963, Johns Hopkins University, 1976). Further, "the problem is more acute in the remote areas, where, whatever meagre facilities have been made available, they are not optimally utilized by the people. Instead, people go to practitioners of indigenous methods". (Working Group, 2000).

Several studies carried on various issues of PHC's, can be grouped under four broad sections. They are:

(i) Organization, administration, infrastructural facilities, interface with referral centres and their sectoral coordination with other developmental programmes.
(ii) Utilization of facilities of Primary Health Centres: providers' and receivers' perspectives and alternatives to the health care system.
(iii) Delivery of various services and its variations at different levels.
(iv) Economic issues related to the services at Primary Health Centres.

Functions of PHC

A. Individual Services

- Medical care
- MCM
- FP
- School Health
- Health Education

B. Community Services

- Prevention and control of endemic diseases
- Environmental sanitation vital statistics
- National health programmes

C. Technical/Managerial Services

- Referral
- Laboratory
- Training
- Office and Management

The above important components and functions does require an adoption of holistic approach applying both accessibility and equity as well as health behaviour criteria in the location of PHC's.

Distribution of PHCs

Locational Planning

One of the main objectives of primary health care policies, particularly for countries with a large, dispersed rural population, is to increase the physical accessibility of the health care facilities provided by the State. This objective derives from the need to improve the availability of basic health services to rural dwellers, and to reduce the inequalities created by a centralized health system which tries to serve a widespread population. Planners often seek to meet this objective by decentralizing the existing health care system so as to provide essential services at the community level with referral to more specialized services through a hierarchy of health centres and hospitals (Godlund, 1961, Massam *et al.*, 1986, Mulvihill, 1991, Rushton, 1991).

However, even if a Government does reallocate resources towards decentralizing and reorganizing a health care system to improve service availability at the community level, it will be impossible to provide every community with a primary health care centre; often it will be a matter of providing one centre to serve a number of communities. Moreover, in most countries some health care facilities already exist in rural areas, and these need to be integrated into a hierarchical system.

Thus, when considering the accessibility of primary health care facilities, policy-makers and planners need to take into account not only the optimum location in terms of accessibility to a number of communities, but also the constraints imposed on the choice of location of existing facilities. Besides there are wide inequalities in the provision of PHCs per lakh of population (Fig. 5.1). Twenty-three PHCs serve one lakh of population in Assam, while only two PHCs serve the same number of people in Punjab. While seven PHCs serve one lakh of population in Himachal Pradesh only three PHCs are available for one lakh population in Uttarakhand. In high population density states of Uttar Pradesh, Madhya Pradesh and Maharashtra, two PHCs each are available for one lakh of population.

These inequalities will have to be removed with the help of locational analysis and health behaviour approach in the spatial distribution of PHCs.

PHC Per Lakh of Population (2004)

Andhra Pradesh	1.95	Mizoram	6.41
Arunachal Pradesh	7.1	Nagaland	4.37
Aasam	22.88	Orissa	3.48
Bihar	1.98	Punjab	1.99
Chhattisgarh	2.48	Rajasthan	2.96
Goa	1.41	Sikkim	4.44
Gujarat	2.11	Tamil Nadu	2.21
Haryana	1.93	Tripura	2.28
Himachal Pradesh	7.21	Uttarakhand	2.7
Jammu & Kashmir	3.29	Uttar Pradesh	2.19
Jharkhand	2.08	West Bengal	1.46
Karnataka	3.18	A & N Islands	5.61
Kerala	2.93	D & N Haveli	2.72
Madhya Pradesh	1.98	Daman & Diu	1.9
Maharashtra	1.84	Lakshadweep	6.59
Manipur	3.32	Pondicherry	4
Meghalaya	4.1		

Source: Based on data from Health Information of India (2005), CBHI, New Delhi

The Geography of Health Care

Geographers are constantly preoccupied with decisions relating to optimum location and optimization of location. In no field is this more important than in the field of medical provision where the cost of facilities, even when inadequate are high. One can see that location is a very important aspect of health services operations, which is the best location for a general health centre or a hospital so as to minimize aggregate travel distance, time and cost? What criteria can be adopted for determining the number of sick beds and the number of physicians in local, regional or national hospitals? Godlund's study in Sweden, using isochrones, is a landmark in this respect (1961). Also noteworthy are the use of location-allocation models in improving the geographical accessibility of rural services by Rushton (1991); access and utilization of public health centres in Guatemala City by Mulvihill (1991); and application of operations research to health planning in Zambia, by Massam, Akhtar and Askew (1991).

According to Hunter (1975), locational planning, whether *de novo* creation of services or contraction or extension of existing services, must take into account:

(1) The scope of the services to be provided (based on disease surveillance and it/s spatial patterns in the locality or in the region);
(2) A realistic view of resources, needs and finance;
(3) The geographical distribution of the population at risk;
(4) The projected population changes through natural increase or decrease and migration; and
(5) Disease forecasting.

Akhtar has added sixth component of health care behaviour, in the locational planning of health care provision (Akhtar, 2000).

Health behaviour may be defined as the process through which a person who perceives himself or herself to be ill, chooses and implements strategies to facilitate the restoration of health. Geographers have studied both the illness and health care behaviour in the framework of socio-economic and cultural dimensions. Stock's study in Nigeria (1987), Good's work on ethno-medicine in Kenya (1989), Gesler's study on health practitioners in Calabar, Nigeria (1979), Bhardwaj's work in Punjab (1975) and Nilofar Izhar's work in Aligarh (1990) are important contributions in health care behaviour.

Methodology

Location Planning

Diesfeld (1974) described the hospital catchment area as a circle/

areas r^2 with the radius r determined by the maximum distance people travel to hospital. He divided the catchment area into three zones*:

- *Zone 1* with an inner radius r, of 10 miles. This covers the distance that people are prepared to walk, if transport is not available.
- *Zone 2* with a middle radius r_1 of 20 miles. This involves the use by patients of public and private transport.
- *Zone 3* a radius r_3 of 30 miles. This zone encompasses the maximum areas from which patients will come to the hospital (Table 5.1):

Table 5.1: The Theoretical Zones of PHC Catchment Areas

	Zone 1	*Zone 2*	*Zone 3*
Radius	n = 10m. (16km)	R_z = 20m. (32km)	R_3 = 30m. (48km)
Zone Area	Z_1=314.159m^2 (814331 km^2)	Z_2=942477m^2 (2441758km^2)	Z_3= 1570795m^2 (4071658 km^2)
Catchment Area	C=Z, =314.159 m^2 (814331 km^2)	C= $Z_1 + Z_2$ =1256636 m^2 (3256089 km^2)	C= $Z_1 + Z_2 + Z_3$ =2827431 m^2 (7327747 km^2)

It is clear from Table 5.2 that these are simply theoretical catchment zones and therefore, cannot be considered as true PHC zones of influence. In fact there are three main factors which determine the functional relationship between the PHC and its surrounding population.

The theoretical zones may be modified by adopting these factors or indicators:

(i) Attractivity of a PHC in terms of size, staffing, equipment and reputation;

(ii) Accessibility in terms of its topographical situation, distance from the next PHC;

(iii) Patients' turnover. This is an important indicator which

* However, such models are applicable basically in homogeneous regions.

actually indicates the size of the PHC catchment area. The total number of in-patients and out-patients registered with each PHC must be taken into account to formulate this indicator.

Table 5.2: Distribution of Score Values for various Indicators

Attractiveness	*Score*
Number of doctors	4
More than 3 (including female doctor)	3
2-3	2
1-2	1
1	
Accessibility	Score
Distance (in km) PHC of next higher priority.	4
More than 50	3
20-50	2
10-20	1
upto 10	
Situation in road net-work:	
At junction	4
At single road	3
At bifurcation from the road (not for)	2
At bifurcation from the main road (far off)	1

Table 5.2 presents score values for various indicators–attractiveness and accessibility which can be utilized in regionalization of PHC services. PHC catchment areas may be identified in order to minimize inequalities in the health care provision.

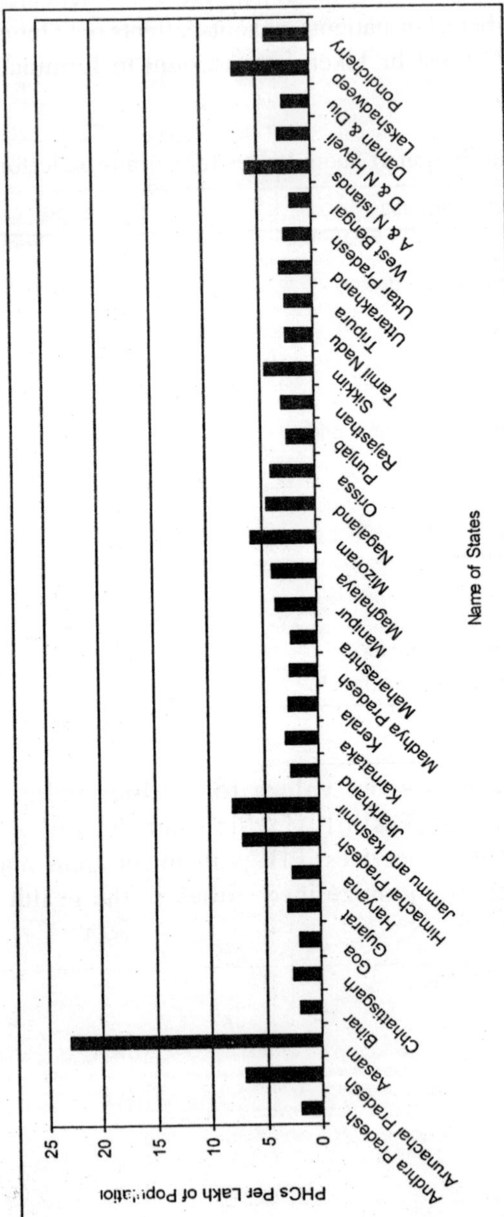

Source: Based on data from Health Information of India (2005), CBHI, New Delhi

Fig. 5.1 Primary Health Centres per Lakh of Population (by States) (2004)

REFERENCES

Akhtar, R. (1991). *Health Care Patterns and Planning in Developing Countries,* Greenwood Press, New York, XI.

Akhtar, R. (2000). A plea for health care behaviour research in India, In A.G. Noble *et al.*, (eds) *Geographic and Planning Research Themes for the New Millennium,* Vikas, New Delhi, 339-48.

Bhardwaj, S. M. (1975). Attitude towards different systems of medicine: A survey of four villages in Punjab. *Social Science and Medicine,* 9, 603-612.

Diesfeld, H.J. (1974). The definition of the hospital catchment area and its population as a denominator for the evaluation of hospital returns in developing countries, *International Journal of Epidemiology,* 247-53.

Gesler, W.M. (1979). Illness and health practitioner use in Calabar, Nigeria, *Social Science and Medicine,* 13D, 23-30.

Godlund, S. (1961). *Population, Regional Hospitals, Transport Facilities, and Regions,* Lund Studies in Geography, No. 21 Series B. Human Geography.

Good, C.M. (1989). *Ethnomedical Systems in Africa,* New York, Guildford.

Griffith, (1963). Quoted from *Primary Health Care in India,* the Working Group on Primary Health Care, Tata Institute of Social Sciences, Mumbai, 2000.

Hunter, J. M. (1974). The challenge of medical geography. In J. M. Hunter (ed) *The Geography of Health and Disease,* University of North Carolina, Chapel Hill X, 11, 6, 15.

Izhar, I. (1990). Patient's origins and usage of a unani clinic in Aligarh Town, India, *Social Science and Medicine,* 30, 1139-41.

Johns Hopkins University (1976). Quoted from *Primary Health Care in India, op. cit.*

Massam. B. H., Akhtar, R., and Askew, I.D. (1991). Applying operations research to health planning. Locating health centres in Zambia, In R. Akhtar (ed) *op cit.,* 183-196.

Mulvihill, J.L. (1991). The access andutilization of public health centers in Guatemala city, in R. Akhlar (ed.) *op. cit,* 171-182.

Rushtan, G. (1991). Use of location-allocation models for improving the geographical accessibility of rural services in developing countries. In R. Akhtar (ed) *Health Care Patterns and Planning in Developing Countries.* Greenwood Press, New York, 147-170.

Smith, D.M. (1979). *Where the Grass is Greener: Geographical Perspectives on Inequality,* Croom Helm, London, p.11.

Stock, R. (1987). Understanding health care behaviour: A model together with evidence from Nigeria. In R. Akhtar (ed) *Health and Disease in Tropical Africa: Geographical and Medical Viewpoints,* Harwood Academic Publisher, London, 279-92.

Working Group on Primary Health Care (2000). *Primary Health Care in India.* Draft Documents, Tata Institute of Social Sciences, Mumbai.

6

Health Care Development in Jammu and Kashmir

In the last fifty years, a lot of progress has taken place in health care infrastructure in Jammu and Kashmir. Total number of Medical Institutions in the State increased from 124 in 1950-51 to 905 in 1970-71 and 3,692 in 2000-01. Percentage increase during 1950 51 and 2000-01 is 2,877 (Table 6.1. Fig. 6.1).

Population-Medical Institution ratio is an important indicator of progress on health care delivery pattern. In 1950-51, 26,242 persons were dependent on one medical institution. With the increase in the number of medical institutions; the Population-Medical Institution ratio was reduced to 3,290 in 1980-81 and 2,727 in 2000-01. Bed strength in hospital and dispensary is another important indicator of health care development. In 1950-51, there were 1,472 beds which increased to 5,422 in 1980-81 and 11,481 in 2000-01. It is evident that the increase in the number of beds has not been substantial, as a number of dispensaries were established without inpatient bed provision. Bed population ratio which was 2,292 in 1950-51 declined to 1,102 in 1980-81 and 877 in 2000-01.

Table 6.1 also reveals that there has been a substantial increase in the number of medical practitioners during 1950-51 and 2000-01. There were only 184 medical practitioners in the State of Jammu and Kashmir in 1950-51. This figure of 184 increased to 2,192 in 1980-81, and 4,774 in 2000-01.

Table 6.1: Health Care Development in Kashmir 1950-51—2000-01

	Medical Institution	*Population per Medical Institution*	*Bed Strength in Hospital and Dispensary*	*Population per Bed*	*Doctors, Vaids & Hakims in Hospital*	*Population per Doctor, Vaid & Hakim*
1950-51	124	26,242	1,472	2,292	184	17,684
1960-61	401	8,560	2,829	1,259	557	6,393
1970-71	905	5,101	4,228	1,092	1,365	3,382
1980-81	1,816	3,290	5,422	1,102	2,192	2,726
1988-89	3,186	2,306	7,479	982	2,788	2,635
2001-02	3,692	2,727	11,481	877	4,774	2,109

Source: Indicators of Economic Development: Jammu and Kashmir 1988-89, Directorate of Economics and Statistics, Government of J&K, Srinagar, 1989 and Digest of Statistics, Directorate of Economics and Statistics, Government of J&K, 2003.

Population practitioner ratio stands at 17,684 in 1950-51 declined substantially to 2,726 in 1980-81, and 2,109 in 2000-01.

To sum up, it looks as there has been an overall development in the provision of health care facilities in the State of Jammu and Kashmir. However, when data are analyzed spatially, inequalities clearly emerged indicating the spatial pattern in over-served and underserved areas. Attempt has been made to prepare health care distribution maps using district as a unit. The basic objective is to demonstrate inequalities in the health care provision of Jammu and Kashmir State.

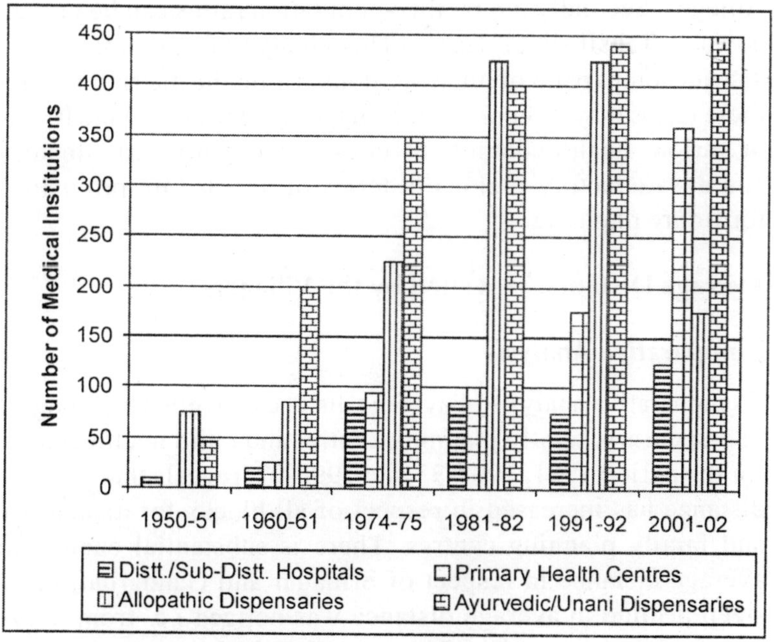

Source: Based on data obtained from Digest of Statistics 2001.

Figure 6.1: Medical Institutions in Jammu and Kashmir

Health Care Services in Jammu and Kashmir

A Question of Equity

The study used medical institution-population ratio, doctor-population ratio and bed-population ratio for demarcating inequalities in their distribution. These ratios should serve distinct purposes. At district level, it provides a measure by which spatial pattern in health care facilities in J and K and may be compared nationally. In the context of doctors, this method has implication with regard to the requirement and the supply of medical graduates from Jammu and Srinagar medical colleges. Secondly the facility-population ratios can be broken down to Tehsil/Block levels. This change of scale allows the district comparison of micro-regions within the district. Finally these ratios may be compared with the standard set by the ICMR or various health committees in order to identify satisfactory and unsatisfactory regions in terms of health care provisions for future planning.

Average Distance Travelled by the Villagers

Comparative Analysis

A comparative analysis of average distance travelled by villagers to dispensary, family planning centre, and child health centre, for the period 1981, 1994-95 and 1996-97, reveals that average distance has increased in respect of all blocks for dispensary and family planning centres. There is substantial change in average distance in respect of Srinagar and Ganderbal, but a steep decline in average distance was noticed *i.e.* from 33.01 kms. to 4.46 kms. and 46.75 kms. to 7.50 kms. in respect of Lar and Kangan blocks. Thus it can be said that more and more child health centres were opened in mostly rural areas. It can be said that average distances have increased during the period of 16 years (*i.e.* 1981-1996-97) in blocks with rapid pace of urbanization.

Table 6.2: Average Distance Travelled by the Villagers Comparative Analysis (in kms.)

	Dispensary			*Family Planning Centre*			*Child Health Centre*		
Block	*1981*	*1994-95*	*1996-97*	*1981*	*1994-95*	*1996-97*	*1981*	*1994-95*	*1996-97*
Srinagar	2.24	2.18	2.58	3.36	9.84	13.12	14.11	9.86	12.02
Ganderbal	1.79	1.66	1.75	4.35	5.92	6.12	22.58	21.85	23.55
Lar	1.62	1.62	1.67	2.58	3.23	3.30	33.01	4.51	4.46
Kangan	1.38	1.71	2.47	5.47	6.13	7.55	46.75	6.76	7.50

SPATIAL PATTERNS OF HEALTH CARE FACILITIES BY DISTANCE (BLOCK-WISE STUDY)

Block Srinagar

The distance pattern in respect of dispensary location varies from 0 to 30 kms. Majority of the villages in Srinagar Block are located in the range of 1-4 kms. Faqir Gujree is the only village located at a distance of 30 kms. from a dispensary. Average distance travelled by the villagers is 2.58 kms.

Inequalities also occur in respect of the availability of family planning centre. The distance varies from 4-45 kms, villages Kreshi Bal, Wani Hama, Gassu and Inder Hama are located at the lowest distance of 4 kms. Village Faqir Hama is located at a distance of 45 kms. from family planning centre. Average distance travelled by the villagers is 13.12 km.

The distance pattern in the availability of Child Health Centre varies from 0-45 kms. Villages of Kreshi Bal, Wani Hama and Gassu are the better off villages located at a distance of 4 kms. from Child Health Centre, and Faqir Gujree village is the most inaccessible village, as the villagers had to travel some 45 kms. for Child Health Care Centre. Average distance travelled by the villagers of Srinagar Block comes to 12.02 kms.

Block Ganderbal

The distance pattern in the block Ganderbal varies from 0-8 kms. with the exception of villages Baba Darya Din, Wanihama Bala, and Hakim Gund. All the remaining villages are located no more than 4 kms. from dispensary. Average distance travelled by the villagers to obtain medical care from the dispensary comes to 1.75 kms. With reference to the location of Family Planning Centre the distance pattern varies between 0-14 kms. Barring village Tullmullah, where one Family Planning Centre is located followed by village Saloora, located at a distance of 1 km, most of the villages are located more than 5 kms. away from Family Planning Centre. Villages Hadorah and Wanihama Bala are located at a distance of 14 kms, the largest distance covered by the villagers for the Family Planning Centre. Average distance travelled by the villagers to the Family Planning Centre comes to 6.12 kms.

However, the distance increases in respect of the availability of Child Health Centre. The distance varies from 10-33 kms, with village Gotli Bagh located at a distance of 33 kms. from the Child Health Centre. Village Baqra is the only village where Child Health Centre facility is accessible at lowest distance *i.e.* 10 kms. Average distance travelled by the villagers to Child Health Centre comes to 23.55 kms.

Block Kangan (1996-97)

The distance pattern for the dispensaries in the block varies from 0-15 kms. with the exception of village Saraf Raw and Hari Ganwan where the dispensary is located at distance of about 15 and 12 kms. respectively, most of the villages have location of dispensary not more than 5 kms. away from the settlement. The average distance travelled by the villagers comes to 2.43 kms. The analyses the distance pattern for Family Planning Centres in the block, figures reveal that apart from the villages of Nilgrar, Sonamarg, Porajat Garjangair, Kullen, Ravel, Gundserring, Fraw Haknar, Sumbal Bala, Soraf Raw, Hari Ganwan where the Family Planning Centres are located between the distance range of 12-23 kms., most of the other villages have these centres located not more than 8 kms. away from the settlement. The average distance travelled by the villagers to Family Planning Centre comes to 7.55 kms. Likewise looking at the distance pattern of Child Health Centres, almost similar pattern emerges. Except the above mentioned villages which have Child Health Centres located in the distance range of 12-23 kms., the remaining villages have these centres located at distance not more than 8 kms. away from the settlement. Average distance travelled to obtain medical care at the Child Health Centre comes to 7.50 kms.

Block Lar (1996-97)

The distance pattern for dispensaries in the block varies from 0-7 kms. With the exception of villages Latiwaza and Baba Salina located at distance of 6 and 7 kms. respectively, most of the villages have the dispensaries located at not more than 5 kms. away from the settlement. Average distance travelled by the villagers comes to 1.67 kms. The distribution of Family Planning Centres shows that the distance pattern varies from 0-9 kms. With the exception of Wata Lar, Bonizal and Latiwaza located at distance of 9, 8 and 8 kms. respectively, most of the villages are not more than 5 kms. away from the settlement with 24 villages having the Family Planning Centres located between 3-7 kms. range. Average distance travelled by the villagers comes to be 3.30 kms. For the Child Health Centre, the distance pattern varies from 0-12 kms. Villages Arhama and Anderwan have Child Health Centres farthest from the settlements at distance of 10 and 12 kms. respectively, while rest are not located farther than 9 kms. Average distance travelled by the villagers comes to 4.46 kms.

HEALTH CARE SERVICES IN JAMMU AND KASHMIR

A Question of Equity

The study used medical institution-population ratio, doctor-population ratio and bed-population ratio for demonstrating inequalities in their distribution. These ratios should serve two distinct purposes. At district level, it provides a measure by which spatial pattern in health care facilities in J & K may be compared nationally. In the context of doctors, this method has implication with regard to the requirement and the supply of medical graduates from Jammu and Srinagar medical colleges. Secondly the facility-population ratios can be broken down to Tehsil/Block levels. This change of scale allows the district comparison of micro-regions within the district. Finally these ratios may be compared with the standard set by the ICMR in order to identify satisfactory and unsatisfactory regions in terms of health care provisions for future planning.

Average Distance Travelled by the Villagers

Comparative Analysis

Table 6.3: Average Distance Travelled by the Villagers: Comparative Analysis (in kms.)

Block	*Dispensary*			*Family Planning Centre*			*Child Health Centre*		
	1981	*1994-95*	*1996-97*	*1981*	*1994-95*	*1996-97*	*1981*	*1994-95*	*1996-97*
Srinagar	2.24	2.18	2.58	3.36	9.84	13.12	14.11	9.86	12.02
Ganderbal	1.79	1.66	1.75	4.35	5.92	6.12	22.58	21.85	23.55
Lar	1.62	1.62	1.67	2.58	3.23	3.30	33.01	4.51	4.46
Kangan	1.38	1.71	2.47	5.47	6.13	7.55	46.75	6.76	7.50

A comparative analysis of average distance travelled by villagers to dispensary, Family Planning Centre, and Child Health centre for the period 1981, 1994-95 and 1996-97, reveals that average distance has increased in respect of all blocks for dispensary and Family Planning Centre. There is substantial change in average distance in respect of Srinagar and Ganderbal, but a steep decline in average distance was noticed *i.e.* from 33.01 kms. to 4.46 kms. and 46.75 kms. to 7.50 kms. in respect of Lar and Kangan blocks. Thus it can be said that more and more Child Health Centres were opened in mostly rural areas. It can be said that average distances have increased during the period of 16 years (*i.e.* 1981-1996-97) in blocks with rapid pace of urbanization.

Spatial Pattern of Medical Institutions

1971 Scenario

The distribution pattern of medical institutions per lakh of population in 1971 varied in different districts of the three natural regions. The lowest ratio *i.e.* below 15 per lakh of population is available in most of the districts of the valley of Kashmir-Anantnag, Pulwama, and Srinagar and Jammu district of Jammu region. Between 15 and 20 Medical Institutions per lakh of population are available in the districts of Rajouri and Punch of Jammu region and Baramullah and Kupwara of the valley of Kashmir. Rest of the districts Leh and Kargil of Ladakh region and Doda, Udhampur, and Kathuwa districts of Jammu region possess more than 20 Medical Institutions per lakh of population. The declining ratio and sparse population in the Ladakh region could have increased the population-Medical Institution ratio (Figure 6.2).

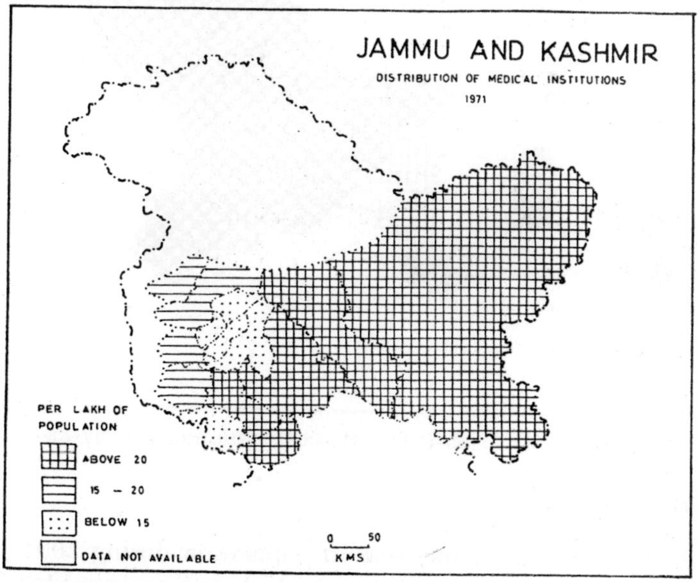

Figure 6.2: Distribution of Medical Institutions (1971)

1987-88 Scenario

The spatial distribution pattern of Medical facilities changes during 1987-88 after a gap of almost sixteen to seventeen years. Besides Ladakh region, Kathuwa, Punch and Rajouri districts of Jammu region possess more than 200 Medical Institutions per lakh of population. However, with the exception of Kupwara district, all other districts of the valley of Kashmir possess less than 50 Medical Institution per lakh of population. The remaining districts, particularly, Doda, Udhampur and Jammu possess between 50-200 Medical Institutions per lakh of Population (Figure 6.3).

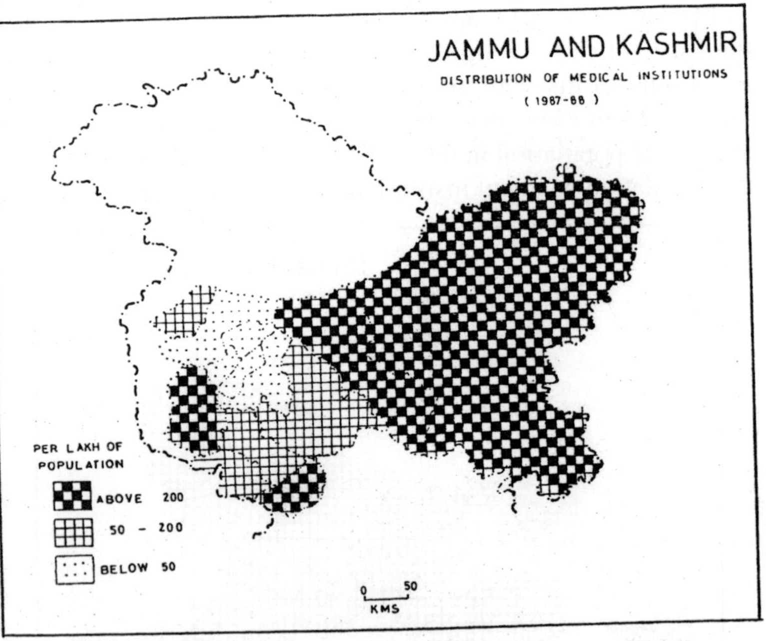

Figure 6.3: Distribution of Medical Institutions (1987-88)

2001 Scenario

With the tremendous increase in population during 2001, the population medical institution ratio declined considerably. This was mainly because the growth in population was far too high than the growth in medical institutions. Besides, a number of dispensaries were closed down and other medical institution became non-functional particularly after 1990s due to turmoil in the valley (Figure 6.4).

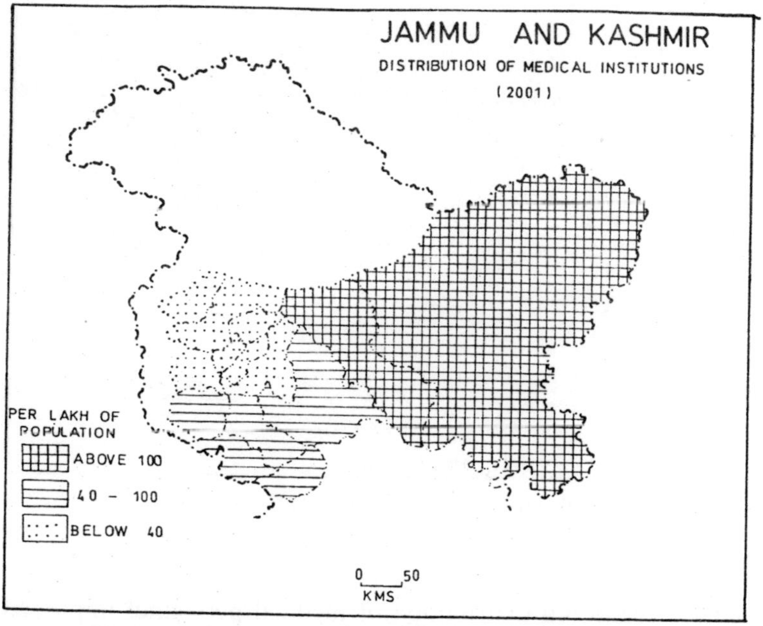

Figure 6.4: Distribution of Medical Institutions (2001)

Spatial Distribution of Medical Personnel

1971 Scenario

Since 1971 a lot of development has taken place as regards the distribution of Medical Personnel while only one district *i.e.* Srinagar possesses 10 and more medical personnel per lakh of population in 1971 and district Jammu acquired a second place with 5-10 medical personnel per lakh of population. Rest of the districts were having less than 5 medical personnel per lakh of population (Figure 6.5).

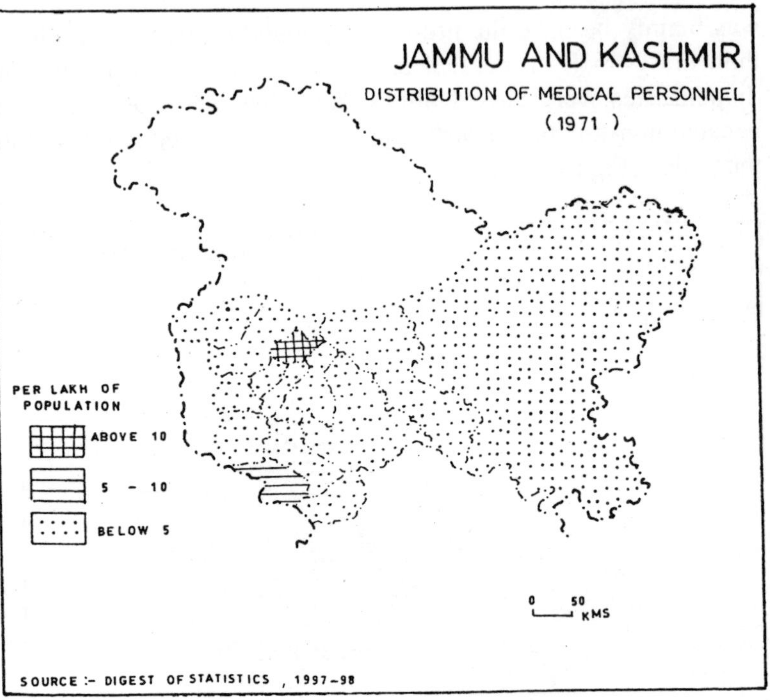

Figure 6.5: Distribution of Medical Personnel (1971)

1987-88 Scenario

Scenario regarding distribution of medical personnel improved considerably in 1987-88. In terms of population medical-personnel ratio situation improved particularly in Leh and Kargil in Ladakh region and Pulwama district of the valley of Kashmir. More than 50 personnel per lakh of population were available in the Leh, Kargil and Pulwama districts. Due to increased population in Jammu and Srinagar districts, being winter and summer capitals of the State of Jammu and Kashmir, about 20-50 medical personnel per lakh of population were available in these districts (Figure 6.6).

2001 Scenario

Figure 6.7 shows the distribution of Medical Personnel in the State

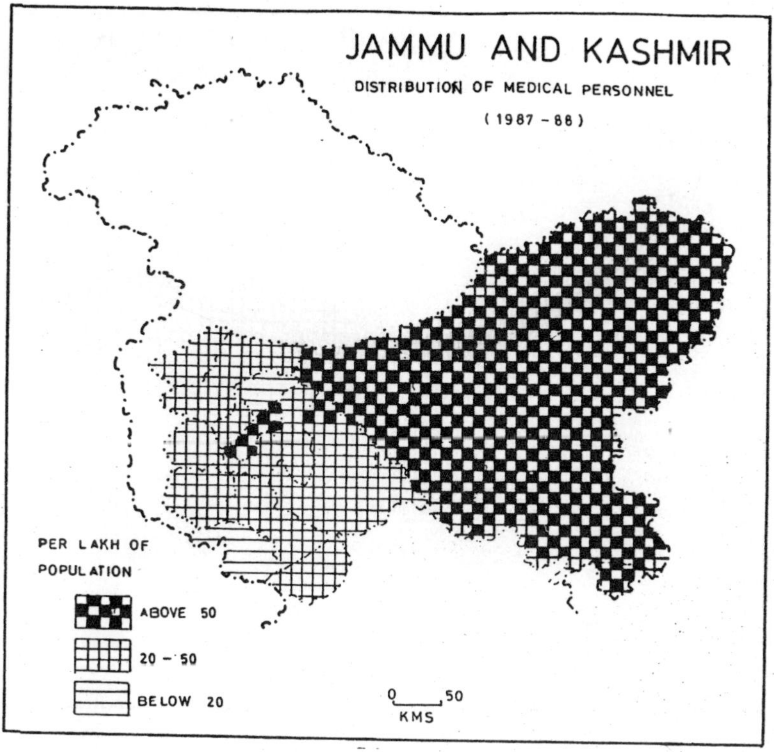

Figure 6.6: Distribution of Medical Personnel (1987-88)

of Jammu and Kashmir. Leh district of Ladakh region and Doda district of Jammu region possess above 45 medical personnel per lakh of population. In all the districts of Kargil in Ladakh region and Anantnag, Pulwama and Budgam districts of the valley of Kashmir the ratio is 20-35 medical personnel per lakh of population. Srinagar, Baramulla and Kupwara districts of the valley of Kashmir possess below 20 medical personnel per lakh of population. The analysis of data shows that neither the population of the district nor the physiographic criteria have been adopted to the provision of Health Care Facilities in the State of Jammu and Kashmir (Figure 6.7).

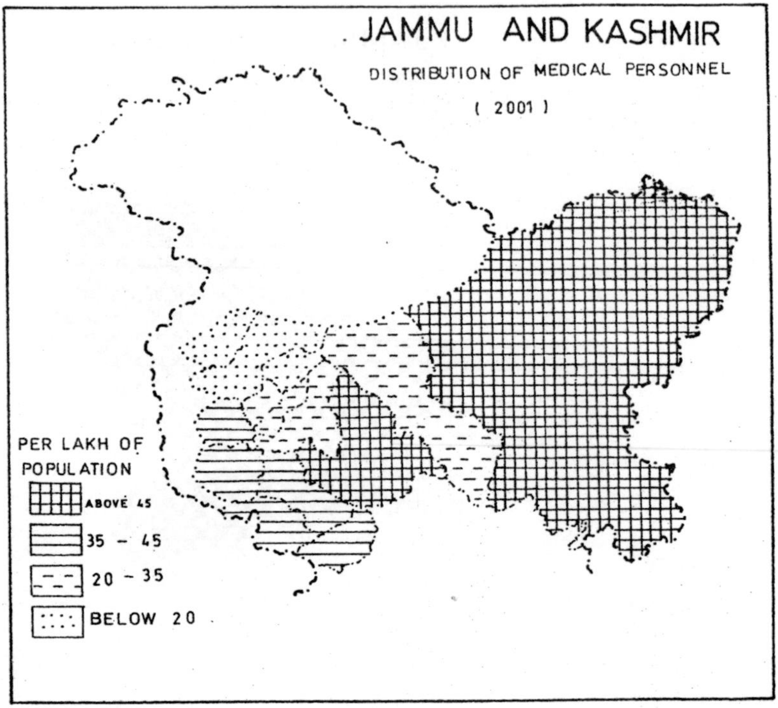

FIG.12

Figure 6.7: Distribution of Medical Personnel (2001)

Spatial Pattern of Beds

1971 Scenario

Figure 6.8 shows the spatial distribution of beds in different Medical Institutions in 1971 in Jammu and Kashmir districts. District Jammu and Srinagar possess more than 100 beds per lakh of population, followed by Leh district with 50-100 beds. Rest of the districts of Jammu and Kashmir regions possess below 50 beds per lakh of population.

1987-88 Scenario

Spatial distribution of beds in 1987-88 reveals that with increased

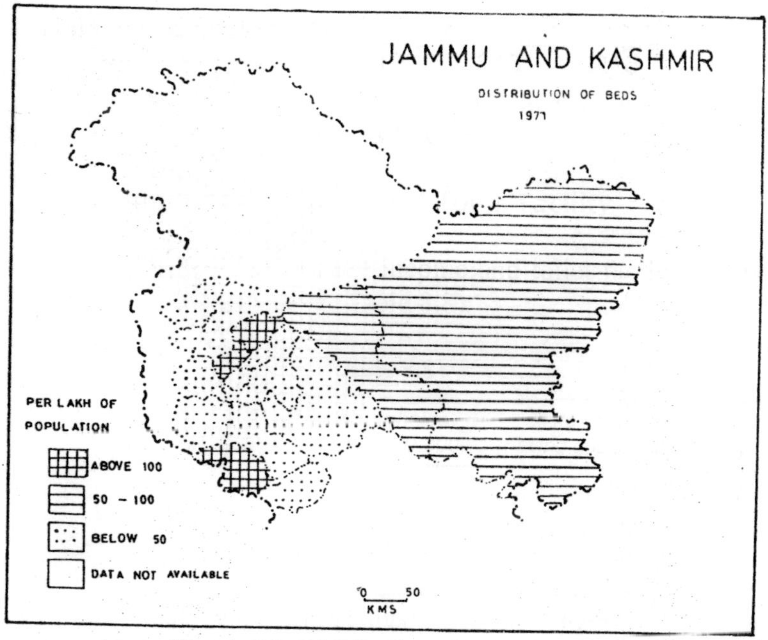

Figure 6.8: Distribution of Beds (1971)

population, since 1971, the bed/population ratio has only slightly improved. However, there is a decline in bed/population ratio in Jammu district. Districts Leh and Kargil of Ladakh region have improved bed/population ratio with above 100 beds per lakh of population (Figure 6.9).

2001 Scenario

More or less similar pattern emerged in the distribution of beds in different districts of Jammu and Kashmir. Leh and Kargil districts of Ladakh possess above 100 beds per lakh of population. All the districts of Jammu region, as well as Pulwama, Budgam and Srinagar districts of the valley of Kashmir possess 50 to 100 beds per lakh of population. The lowest figure *i.e.* below 50 beds per lakh of population was scored in the districts of Anantnag, Baramulla and Kupwara districts of the valley of Kashmir. There is clear evidence of regional inequality in the provision of beds in Jammu and Kashmir (Figure 6.10).

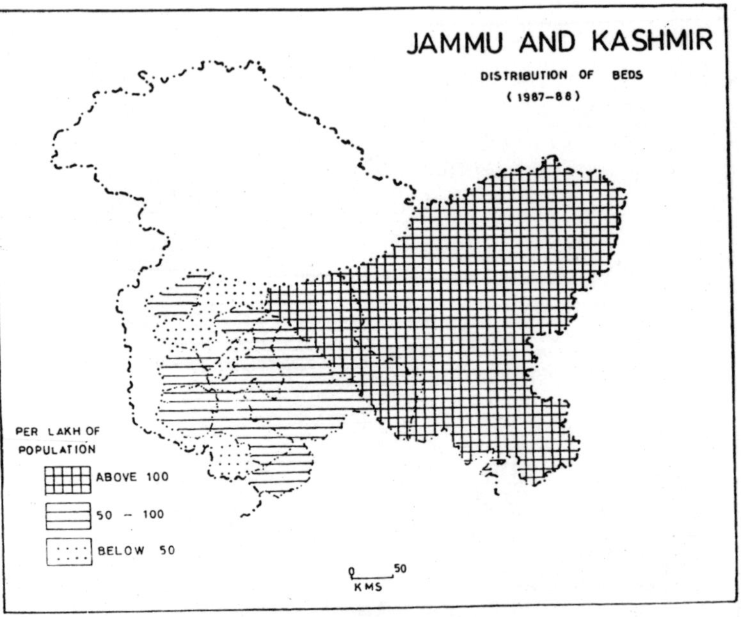

Figure 6.9: Distribution of Beds (1987-88)

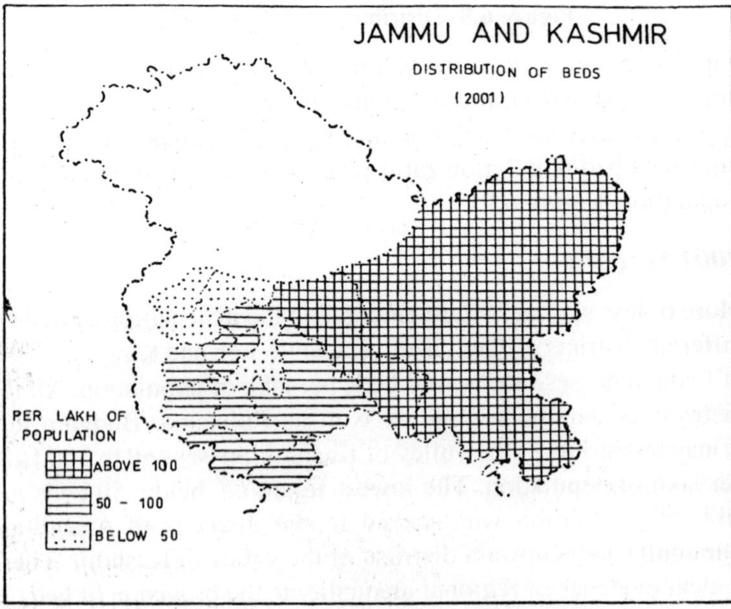

Figure 6.10: Distribution of Beds (2001)

Medical Institutions

Sub-District Hospital

Spatial distribution of sub-district hospitals during 1997-98 shows wide disparities. More than 20 per cent of the total facilities are located in Srinagar district followed by Jammu district. Less than 3 per cent of the total sub-district hospitals are located in Kargil district. Districts Leh, Kupwara and Punch comprise 3-5 per cent of sub-district hospitals. Most of the districts of valley of Kashmir and Jammu region comprise 5-10 per cent of the total sub-district hospitals (Figure 6.11).

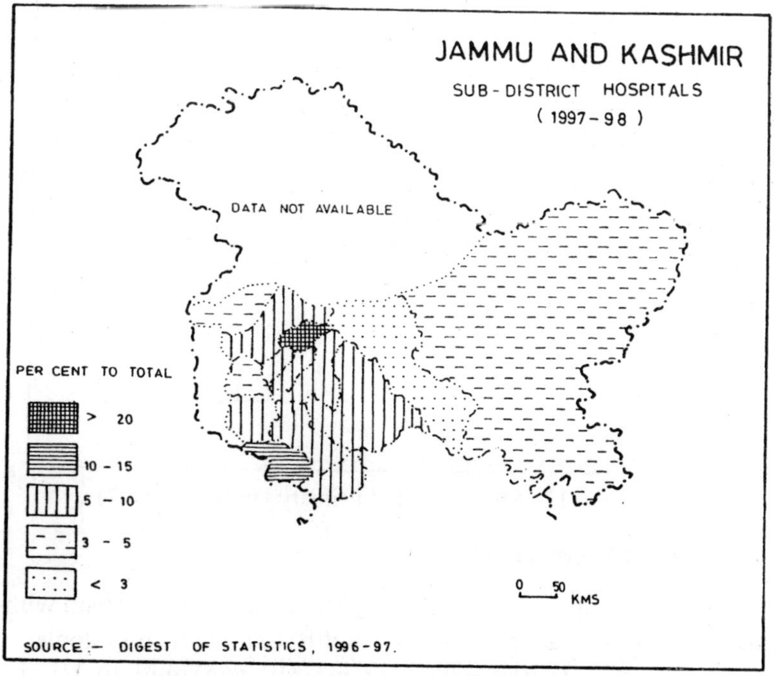

Figure 6.11: Sub-District Hospitals (1997-98)

Allopathic and Primary Units

Distribution of allopathic and primary units (1996-97) reveal a different scenario in the State. Doda district of Jammu region possess more than 13 per cent of the total allopathic and primary units, followed by Udhampur of Jammu region and Srinagar, Baramulla districts with 10-13 per cent of these facilities. Leh district with only less than 3 per cent of the such facilities, require more allopathic and primary units due to the rugged topography and scattered settlement patterns (Figure 6.12).

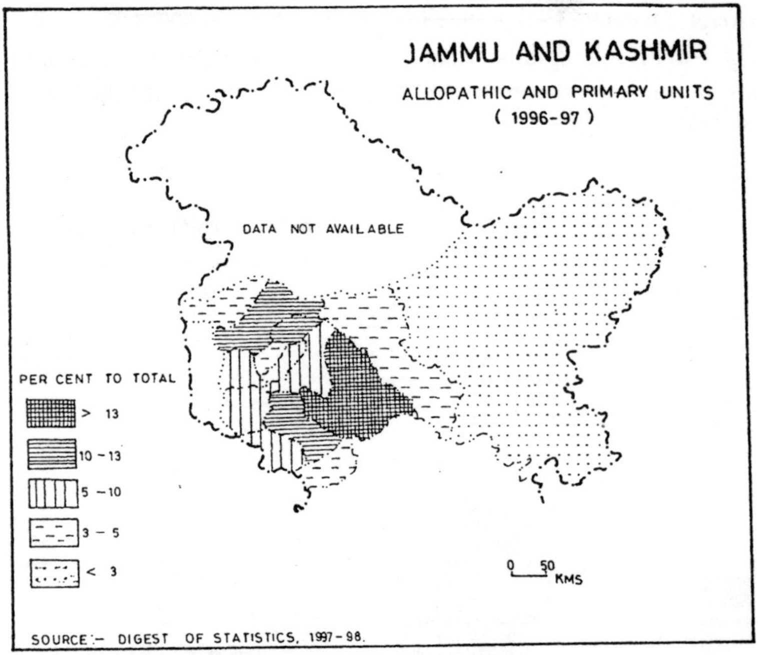

Figure 6.12: Allopathic and Primary Units (1996-97)

Ayurvedic Dispensaries

Jammu and Kashmir is good examples of Medical pluralism with three physiographic regions possess different medical systems.

Ayurvedic dispensaries are mainly confined to Hindu dominated Jammu region with more than 20 per cent of the total Ayurvedic dispensaries, followed by 10-20 per cent in Kathua and Udhampur districts. Muslim dominated Rajouri and Punch districts of Jammu region possess 5-10 per cent of the total Ayurvedic dispensaries (Figure 6.13) (Photographs 6.1 and 6.2).

Photo 6.1

Photo 6.2

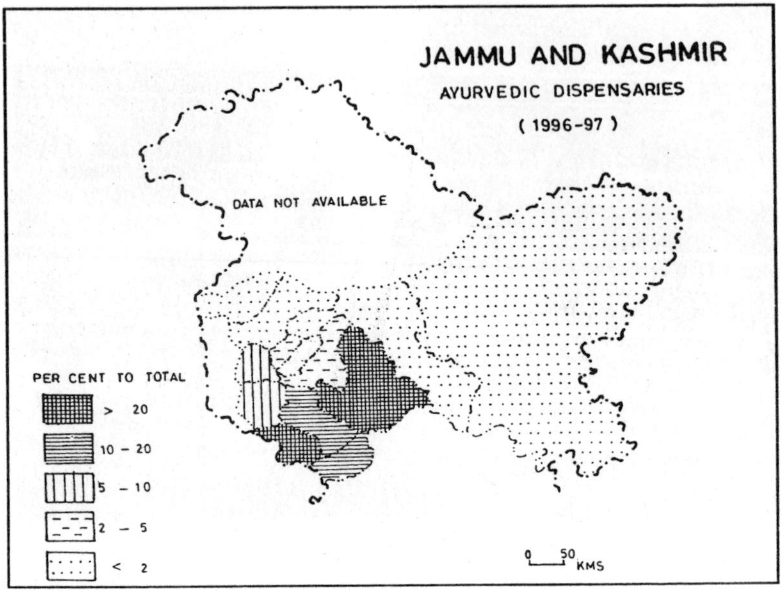

Source: Digest of Statistics, 1996-97.

Figure 6.13: Ayurvedic Dispensaries (1996-97)

Unani Dispensaries

Unani medical system is traditionally most popular among Muslims. Most of the Unani dispensaries are located in the districts in the valley of Kashmir particularly Baramulla, Srinagar, Budgam, Pulwama and Anantnag districts. Doda districts of Jammu region and Kupwara district of valley of Kashmir possess 5-10 per cent of total Unani dispensaries of the State (Photo 6.3). In Leh and Kargil districts of Ladakh region, traditional AMCHI medicine is most popular (Photo 6.4), and Kathua, Jammu and Udhampur districts of Jammu region together comprise less than 2 per cent of the total Unani dispensaries (Figure 6.14).

Photo 6.3

Photo 6.4

Scope of Traditional Medical Systems

The importance of traditional medicine can not be denied since vast majority of population in rural as well as urban areas increasingly rely on the indigenous system of medicine. Attempts should be made to conduct health care behaviour surveys and based upon the results more Ayurvedic and Unani dispensaries be located in the Jammu and Kashmir regions. Amchi dispensaries should also be provided in Ladakh region, particularly in the remotely located villages.

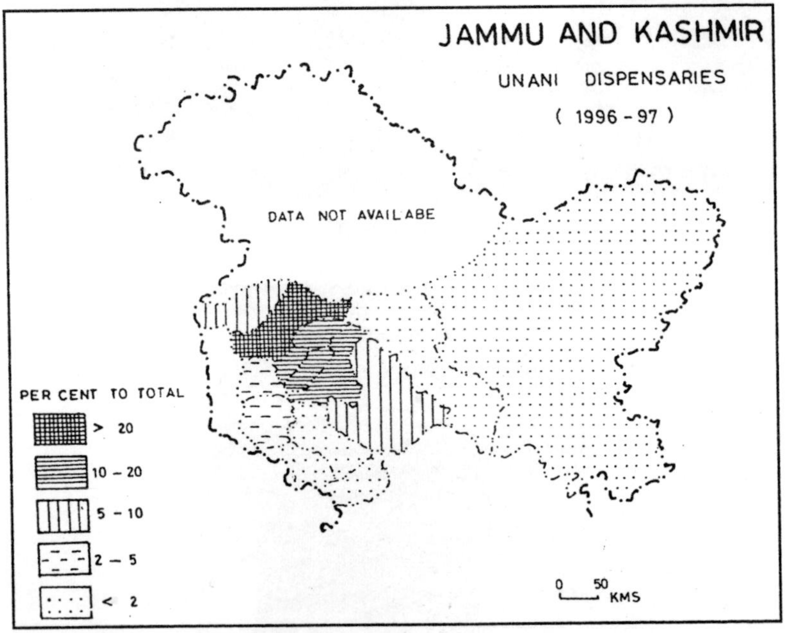

Source: Digest of Statistics, 1996-97.

Figure 6.14: Unani Dispensaries (1996-97)

7

Socio-Cultural, Economic and Health Conditions of Rural Areas of District Jammu

Socio-cultural and economic framework determines health conditions of the population. So far as the religion of the respondents of the surveyed areas of outer Jammu consisting of areas like R.S. Pura, Akhnoor, Purmandal, Purkhoo and Kheri is concerned, some 87.5 per cent of the people are Hindus, 10.41 per cent are Sikhs whereas a negligible portion of the population happens to be Muslims with a percentage of 1.04 whereas 2.08 per cent of the people belong to religions other than the above mentioned religions. Table 7.1 makes it clear that a majority of the people in the peripheral areas of Jammu are Hindus.

Table 7.1: Religion

Village	*Hindu*	*Muslim*	*Sikh*	*Others*
R.S. Pura	12	—	5	—
Purkhoo	18	—	1	—
Akhnoor	15	1	3	1
Purmandal	20	—	—	—
Kheri	19	—	1	—
Total	84	1	10	1
Percentage	87.5	1.04	10.41	2.08

Occupational structure is an important socio-economic parameter. In the peripheral areas half of the respondents (50%) consisted of the service class, whereas 25 per cent of the people were involved with agricultural activities. While only 5 per cent of the people were involved with some sort of business and the remaining 20 per cent were daily wagers who did not have a permanent source of income throughout the year. Looking at the individual areas, R.S. Pura has the highest number of service class people (70.58 %) whereas Akhnoor has the highest number of agricultural workers (21.50%) while Purmandal has highest number of people involved in some sort of business (35%). (Table 7.2)

Table 7.2: Occupation

Village	*Agriculture*	*Service*	*Business*	*Others*
R.S. Pura	2 (17.76%)	12 (70.58%)	—	3 (17.64%)
Akhnoor	4 (21.05%)	13 (68.42%)	1 (5.26%)	1 (5.26%)
Purkhoo	—	9 (45.00%)	1 (5.00%)	10 (50%)
Purmandal	1 (5%)	7 (35.00%)	7 (35.00%)	11 (55.00%)
Kheri	5 (25.00%)	10 (50.00%)	1 (5.00%)	4 (20.00%)

Looking at the house types of the surveyed areas, 82.30 per cent of the households have *pucca* houses whereas only 17.7 per cent of the households have *kuccha* houses. Kheri has the maximum number of *pucca* houses (95.00%) followed closely by Akhnoor at 89.5 per cent and Purkhoo at 80 per cent. Also so far as the *kuccha* houses are concerned R. S. Pura (29.41 %) and Purmandal (25%) have the most number of *kuccha* houses directly pointing to the low standard of living in these areas. Going by this criteria of measuring the standard of living of a place Kheri appears to have the most number of *pucca* houses and least number of *kuccha* houses (1%) and thereby a better standard of living as it has a better standard of housing, while R.S. Pura appears to have the most number of *kuccha* houses (29.41%) and least number of *pucca* houses (70.58%). (Table 7.3)

Table 7.3: House Type

Village	*Kucha*	*Pucca*
R.S. Pura	5 (29.41%)	12 (70.58%)
Purkhoo	4 (20.00%)	16 (80.00%)
Akhnoor	2 (10.52%)	17 (89.47%)
Purmandal	5 (25.00%)	15 (75.00%)
Kheri	1 (5.00%)	19 (95.00%)
Total	17 (17.70%)	79 (82.29%)

Table 7.4 makes it clear that majority *i.e.* 40.62 per cent of the houses have three rooms followed by 25 per cent of the houses that have two rooms. Hence, 65 per cent of the houses have 2-3 rooms, which also points towards a low to moderate income group in majority of the houses in the surveyed areas. About 6.25 per cent of the households have less than two rooms while 10.41 per cent of the households have 4 and 6 rooms. About 6.25 per cent of the houses have 5 rooms while a negligible 1.04 per cent houses have more than six rooms.

So far as the family structure of the surveyed areas is concerned, it becomes evident that majority *i.e.* 63.82 per cent of the houses have a joint family system, while only 36.17 per cent of the households have a nuclear family structure. So far as the individual areas are concerned, Akhnoor has the highest number of joint families (84.21%), followed by Purmandal (77.77%), Kheri (60%), R.S. Pura (58.82%) and Purkhoo (40%). So far as the most number of nucleated households is concerned, Purkhoo with 60 per cent of the households with nucleated families has the most number of the households in the category followed by R.S. Pura, Kheri, Purmandal and Akhnoor with 41.17, 40, 22.22 and 15.78 per cent respectively, thereby apart from

Purkhoo which has highest nucleated families than the joint families, all the other areas have greater number of joint families in comparison to the nucleated family structure, thereby reflecting a very traditional system of family setting. (Table 7.5)

Table 7.4: Number of Rooms

No. of Rooms	*<2*	*2*	*3*	*4*	*5*	*6*	*>6*
R.S. Pura	1 (5.88%)	4 (23.52%)	7 (41.17%)	3 (17.64%)	—	2 (11.76%)	—
Purkhoo	2 (10.00%)	6 (30.00%)	7 (35.00%)	2 (10.00%)	1 (5.00%)	2 (10.00%)	—
Akhnoor	1 (5.76%)	3 (15.78%)	10 (52.63%)	—	2 (10.52%)	2 (10.52%)	—
Purmandal	2 (10.00%)	4 (20.00%)	7 (35.00%)	3 (15.00%)	2 (10.00%)	2 (10.00%)	—
Kheri	—	7 (35.00%)	8 (40.00%)	2 (10.00%)	1 (5.00%)	2 (10.00%)	—
Total	6 (6.25%)	24 (25.00%)	39 (40.62%)	10 (10.41%)	6 (6.25%)	10 (10.41%)	1 (1.04%)

Table 7.5: Family Structure

Village	*Joint*	*Nucleated*
R.S. Pura	10 (58.82%)	7 (41.17%)
Purkhoo	8 (40.0%)	12 (60.00 %)
Akhnoor	16 (84.21%)	3 (15.78%)
Purmandal	14 (77.77%)	4 (22.22%)
Kheri	12 (60.00%)	8 (40.00%)
Total	60 (63.82%)	34 (36.17%)

When one takes a look at the family size of the surveyed areas, it becomes evident that most of the respondents *i.e.* 35.52 per cent have two children followed closely by 23.68 per cent of the people who have three children, thereby indicating that majority *i.e.* 60 per cent of the families have 2-3 children. (Table 7.6)

Table 7.6: Family Size

No. of Children →	*1*	*2*	*3*	*4*	*>4*
R.S. Pura	3 (17.64%)	8 (47.05%)	2 (11.76%)	1 (5.88%)	1 (5.88%)
Purkhoo	3 (15.00%)	6 (30%)	3 (15%)	3 (15%)	—
Akhnoor	5 (26.31%)	6 (31.57%)	3 (15.76%)	—	—
Purmandal	2 (10%)	1 (5%)	7 (35%)	3 (15%)	4 (20%)
Kheri	1 (5%)	6 (30%)	3 (15%)	2 (10%)	3 (15%)
Total	14 (18.42%)	27 (35.52%)	18 (23.68%)	9 (11.84%)	8 (10.52%)

Table 7.7 makes it clear that almost half (49%) of the households use tap water as a major source of drinking water, followed by 27.08 per cent of the households that use hand pump and the remaining 23.95 per cent people get water from outside like the nearby government tap or the nearby river as they do not have a tap nor the hand pump in their house. This points to the fact that so far as the water facility is concerned in the peripheral areas, the picture is not very satisfactory, and as compared to Jammu city wherein 100 per cent population has access to tap water, in the study area almost half of the population uses hand pump water, public tap water and river water.

Table 7.7: Water Facility (Types of Sources)

Village	*Hand pump*	*Tap H_2O*	*From Outside*
R.S. Pura	16 (94.11%)	—	1 (5.88%)
Purkhoo	—	13 (65%)	7 (35%)
Akhnoor	5 (26.31%)	10 (52.63%)	4 (21.05%)
Purmandal	5 (25%)	13 (65%)	2 (10%)
Kheri	—	11 (55%)	9 (45%)
Total	26 (27.08%)	47 (48.95%)	23 (23.95%)

So far as the bathroom/toilet facility is concerned only 59.4 per cent of the households have a bathroom or toilet facility at home while an appreciable proportion of the population *i.e.* 40.62 per cent do not have a bathroom or toilet facility at home, which is not good especially when one considers having a toilet at home as the basic requisite for a hygienic and healthy living. If one looks at the individual areas which have the maximum number of households without a bathroom/toilet facility at home, than Purmandal tops the list with 55 per cent households being without a facility at home thereby raising serious doubts about the standard of living of these areas. (Table 7.8)

Table 7.8: Bathroom/Toilet Facility

Village	*Bathroom at Home*	*Bathroom Outside the Home*
R.S. Pura	12 (70.58%)	5 (29.41%)
Purkhoo	11 (55%)	9 (45%)
Akhnoor	12 (63.15%)	7 (36.84%)
Purmandal	9 (45%)	11 (55%)
Kheri	13 (65%)	7 (35%)
Total	57 (59.37%)	39 (40.62%)

Table 7.9 clearly points out the fact that the majority of the people living in the surveyed areas belong to low income group, which is evident from the fact that 88.16 per cent of the people have income less than 3000 rupees with 48.4 per cent people having an income of 1000-2000 rupees while another 24.73 per cent people have a meagre income of less than 1000 rupees. Such low income makes it clear why people living in these area have problems related to housing and sanitation which infact are related to income.

So far as income governing the health-seeking behaviour of the people is concerned, there is a direct correlation between the two as greater income means greater access to health care but so far as these peripheral areas are concerned only 40 per cent of the

Table 7.9: Income

Income (Rs.)	*<1000*	*1000-2000*	*2000-3000*	*3000-4000*	*4000-5000*	*>5000*
R.S. Pura	2 (12.5%)	11 (68.75%)	2 (12.5%)	1 (6.25%)	—	—
Purkhoo	1 (5%)	10 (25%)	5 (50%)	4 (20%)	—	—
Akhnoor	3 (15.78%)	10 (52.63%)	3 (15.78%)	1 (5.26%)	2 (10.52%)	—
Purmandal	12 (63.15%)	5 (26.31%)	1 (5.26%)	1 (5.26%)	—	—
Kheri	5 (25.31%)	9 (47.36%)	3 (15.78%)	1 (5.26%)	1 (5.26%)	—
Total	23 (24.73%)	45 (48.38%)	14 (15.05%)	8 (8.60%)	3 (3.22%)	—

people believed that their income governs the health-seeking behaviour while 60 per cent believed that their income did not govern their health-seeking behaviour. But the other way of looking at this would be that as almost all the people living in these areas are low income people, thereby it hardly makes any difference to them so far as seeking health care is concerned as they earn very little to afford good health care (Table 7.10):

Table 7.10: Whether Income Governs Health-Seeking Behaviour

	Yes	*No*
R.S. Pura	5	12
Purkhoo	9	11
Akhnoor	5	14
Purmandal	13	7
Kheri	6	14
Total	38 (39.58%)	58 (64.41%)

So far as distance travelled to a health facility is concerned most of the people *i.e.* 26.01 per cent have to travel a distance of 2-6 km, followed closely by 21.9 per cent of the people who have to travel a distance of 14-20 kms. Also 17.70 per cent each of people are those who have to travel a distance of 10-14 and 30-40 km respectively to have access to a health facility. This clearly indicates that people at large do not have a health facility nearby and have to travel an appreciable distance for access to a health facility. This is in sharp contrast to people living in Jammu city who have a health facility within a much more accessible distance and thereby have greater access to health care facilities. Among the individual areas Purkhoo, Purmandal and Akhnoor seem to be the only three places to have health care facilities. Among the individual areas Purkhoo, Purmandal and Akhnoor seem to be the only three places where 10 per cent, 5 per cent and 5.26 per cent people respectively have to travel a distance of less than 2 km. So far as travelling a large distance for a health facility is concerned then 85 per cent, 90 per cent and 11.76 per cent of the population of Purmandal, Purkhoo and R.S. Pura have to travel 30-40 km. and 11-20 km. each respectively to a health facility. (Table 7.11)

Table 7.11: Distance Travelled to a Health Facility

Distance	*>2*	*2-6 km*	*6-10 km*	*10-14 km*	*14-20 km*	*20-30 km*	*30-40 km*	*>40 km*
R.S. Pura	—	15 (88.23%)	—	—	2 (11.76%)	—	—	—
Purkhoo	1 (5.26%)	—	—	(89.47%)	1 (5.26%)	—	—	
Akhnoor	2 (10%)	—	—	—	18 (90%)	—	—	—
Purmandal	1 (5%)	—	—	—	—	2 (10%)	17 (85%)	—
Kheri	—	10 (50%)	2 (10%)	—	—	8 (40%)	—	—
Total	4 (4.16%)	25 (26.04%)	2 (2.08%)	17 (17.70%)	21 (21.87%)	10 (10.41%)	17 (17.70%)	—

Disease Distribution

As far as disease distribution in the peripheral areas is concerned, seasonal diseases like cough and cold, fever etc. seem to be topping the list of diseases with 22 per cent of the people being affected by them followed by diseases like asthma, eye diseases. Blood pressure, headaches, liver and gynaecological problems follow with 17.25 per cent people being affected by them. While

16.75 per cent people are affected by viral diseases, another 12.5 per cent people are suffering from joint pain and bone problems. While 10.5 per cent people are affected by skin problems, 5.75 per cent people have suffered from malaria and other infections respectively. So far as diseases like diarrhoea, stomach problems and chest problems are concerned they affect a minor proportion of the population affecting 4 per cent, 3.25 per cent and 2 per cent people respectively (Table 7.12).

Conclusion

The survey of the peripheral areas of Jammu like R.S. Pura, Akhnoor, Purkhoo, Purmandal and Kheri illustrates that the people live in a very traditional setting with great differences with Jammu city so far as socio-economic indicators are concerned. While the housing scenario is quite satisfactory with 82 per cent being *Pucca* houses but then 65 per cent of the houses have just 2-3 rooms which goes to show that even though 82 per cent of the houses are made of concrete, they have very little space. To add to this only 59.37 per cent houses have a bathroom/toilet facility at home while the remaining people avail the facility outside their home. Also looking at the income of the peripheral areas it was evident that all the people of the surveyed areas belong to the low income group with 88.16 per cent of the people with an income less than 3000 rupees and none of the respondents had an income more than 5000 rupees which in turn affects other parameters like standard of living, health-seeking behaviour etc. So far as the distance to a health- seeking facility is concerned which the people of the surveyed areas have to cover, then again the figures are not very satisfactory as 67.68 per cent of the people have to travel a distance of 10-40 km. Another disturbing figure that came to the fore in course of the study was that only 48.95 per cent people have access to tap water which is in sharp contrast to the Jammu city where 100 per cent people have access to tap water. The only encouraging figures that came to light were related to the family size with 77.62 per cent people have 1-3 children which is pretty satisfying especially when compared to the other figures and parameters.

Table 7.12: Disease Distribution

Village	*Seasonal*	*Joint pain/bones*	*Viral*	*Skin*	*Stomach*	*Infections*	*Chest*	*Malaria*	*Diarrhoea*	*Heart/Brain*	*Others*
R.S. Pura	17 (22.35%)	10 (13.15%)	15 (19.73%)	6 (7.89%)	2 (2.63%)	1 (1.31%)	—	4 (5.26%)	3 (3.94%)	—	18 (23.68%)
Akhnoor	19 (24.67%)	7 (9.09%)	9 (11.68%)	9 (11.68%)	5 (6.49%)	4 (5.19%)	2 (2.59%)	11 (14.28%)	—	2 (2.59%)	9 (11.68%)
Purkhoo	14 (18.42%)	10 (13.15%)	13 (17.10%)	9 (11.84%)	2 (2.63%)	6 (7.89%)	4 (5.26%)	2 (2.63%)	5 (6.57%)	—	11 (14.47%)
Purmandal	18 (21.17%)	11 (12.94%)	14 (16.47%)	12 (14.11%)	2 (2.35%)	6 (7.05%)	2 (2.35%)	1 (1.17%)	1 (1.17%)	—	18. (21.17%)
Kheri	20 (23.25%)	12 (14.11%)	16 (18.60%)	6 (7.05%)	2 (2.35%)	4 (4.64%)	—	5 (5.81%)	7 (8.13%)	1 (1.17%)	13 (0.15%)
Total	88 (22%)	50 (12.5%)	67 (16.75%)	42 (10.5%)	13 (3.25%)	21 (5.25%)	8 (2%)	23 (5.75%)	16 (4%)	3 (0.75%)	69 (17.25%)

Source: Field Work

A comparison between the villages that were surveyed one comes to believe that Kheri and Akhnoor seem to be better off among the different parameters that were used in the study while R. S. Pura, Purkhoo and Purmandal seem to be having not-so-encouraging figures among all the socio-cultural, economic and health parameters that were studied in course of the study.

8

Socio-Cultural Economic Conditions and Health Care of District Srinagar: Correlation Analysis

Srinagar District: Sample Village and Localities

The concept of relationship between sets of objects and between sets of events is part of everyday experience. Both the physical and social sciences have developed and applied rigorous techniques for testing for correlation with help of statistical methods based on probability. In medical geography, relationships have also frequently been computed associating socio-economic variables and health variables. They have been part of geography for a long time. Indeed the geographer is inclined to see potential causal relationships between any two things that seem to be together in area.

An attempt has been made to study association between literacy rate and percentage of government employees, literacy rate and the use of traditional medicine, unsatisfactory household hygiene, occupation and use of unani medicine, literacy rate and household income, income and use of traditional medicines, and use of allopathic medicine and reporting of side effects.

The Table 8.1 shows the literacy rate and its relation with Government employment. The sample villages and urban localities are Manigam, Tailbal, Rainawari, Dalgate, Shallbug and Khonmoh of Kashmir Valley.

The highest rate falls in Manigam-70 per cent, followed by Shallbug, 63 per cent, Raniwari, 50 per cent, Delgate and Khonmoh 40 per cent each. The lowest literacy rate was found in Tailbal. The highest percentage of Government employees was found in Manigam *i.e.* 57 per cent followed by Rainawari, 30 per cent, Tailbal 20 per cent, Khonmoh 17 per cent and Shallbug (13%).

The literacy rate in all six sample villages is higher than the percentage of Government employee. There is no effect of distance factor. Dalgate which is near to the core area of Srinagar city has no share in Government employment. Manigam, having highest percentage of both literacy rate and Government employment, is far from Srinagar city.

The coefficient of correlation between the two variables is 0.38 which indicates the positive correlation.

Table 8.2 shows the literacy rate and its relation with household hygienc. The sample villages are Manigam, Tailbal, Rainawari, Dalgate, Shallbug and Khonmoh of Srinagar district. The highest literacy rate is found in Manigam and Shallbug with 70 and 63 per cent respectively. These two villages have high level of household hygiene (57%). The highest household hygiene conditions were found in Tailbal which has the lowest literacy rate (33%).

Thus it may be concluded that the two variables are negatively correlated (-0.05), hence there is no interdependence of the two variables.

Table 8.3 shows the literacy rate and its relation with usage of traditional medicine. The highest literacy rate in all six sample villages was found in Manigam with zero percentage usage of traditional medicine. The lowest literacy rate was found in Tailbal (33%) with highest usage of traditional medicine. Khonmoh with 40 per cent of literacy rate has 17 per cent of usage of traditional medicines. The other three villages Rainawari, Dalgate and Shallbug have zero per cent usage of traditional medicine.

The coefficient of correlation is -0.48 which means that there is no interdependence of the two variables.

Table 8.4 depicts the relation between labour workforce and usage of traditional medicines. The highest labour work occupation falls in Khonmoh (50%) followed by Tailbal (37%), Manigam and Rainawari with 30 per cent each. The lowest labour-work occupation was found in Dalgate and Shallbug with 20 per cent each. The highest usage of traditional medicines was found in Tailbal *i.e.* 17 per cent followed by Khonmoh (13%). In other four villages viz. Manigam, Rainawari, Dalgate and Shallbug people do not use traditional medicines.

The co-efficient of correlation between the two variables is 0.82.

Table 8.5 shows the relationship between literacy rate and labour workforce. The sample villages Manigam, Tailbal, Rainawari, Dalgate, Shallbug and Khonmoh are either within or nearby Srinagar city. The highest literacy rate was found in Manigam *i.e.* 70 per cent with 30 per cent labour workforce while the highest labour workforce was found in Khonmoh *i.e.* 50 per cent with 40 per cent literacy rate. The lowest labour-workforce was found in Dalgate and Shallbug with 20 per cent each with 40 and 60 per cent literacy rate respectively.

The coefficient of correlation between the two variables is -0.37 which indicates the negative correlation.

Table 8.6 reveals the relation between income range (1600-3000) and labour workforce with 50 per cent people of Khonmoh in the above income group which is the highest in all sample villages and localities, besides the highest labour force *i.e.* 50 per cent also in Khonmoh village. The lowest labour workforce *i.e.* 20 per cent falls in Dalgate and Shallbug with 40 and 73 per cent of above income class respectively. The other two villages Manigam and Tailbal comprises 30 per cent population with income group 1600-3000 and with 30 and 37 per cent labour workforce respectively.

The coefficient of correlation is 0.08.

Table 8.7 reveals the relationship between 1600-3000 income class and share of rooms (5-8). The highest percentage of this income category falls in Khonmoh *i.e.* 50 per cent followed by Dalgate (40%), Shallbug (37%), Manigam and Tailbal (30% each). The lowest percentage of this income group falls in Rainawari *i.e.* 23%. The highest share of rooms (5-8) falls in Dalgate *i.e.* 63% followed by Tailbal and Rainawari (30% each). The lowest share of (5-8) rooms falls in Khonmoh (20%), Shallbug (17%) and Manigam (10%).

The coefficient of correlation is 0.07 which indicates slightly positive correlation between the two variables.

Table 8.8 shows the relation between income class (1600-3000) and good toilet facilities. The highest share of this income falls in Khonmoh *i.e.* 50 per cent followed by Dalgate (boat population) (40%), Shallbug (37%), Manigam and Tailbal (30% each) and Rainawari (23%), The highest percentage of good toilet facilities falls in Dalgate (73%), Rainawari (67%), Manigam (53%), Tailbal (30%), Shallbug (27%) and Khonmoh (23%).

The coefficient of correlation between the two variables is -0.37.

Table 8.9 reveals the relation between income class (1600-3000) and usage of traditional medicine. The highest percentage of usage of traditional medicines falls in Tailbal (17%) followed by Khonmoh (13%). The other four sample villages and localities *i.e.* Manigam, Rainawari, Dalgate (boat population) and Shallbug have zero per cent share of the usage of traditional medicines. The highest percentage of above income class falls in Khonmoh (50%) followed by Dalgate (boat population) (40%), Shallbug (37%), Manigam and Tailbal (30%) each, and Rainawari (23%).

The coefficient of correlation between the two variables is 0.31.

Table 8.10 reveals the relation between the two variables viz. usage of traditional medicine and side effects. The cent per cent usage of traditional medicine is found in Shallbug followed by Tailbal (90%), Rainawari (73%), Manigam and Khonmoh (63% each) and Dalgate (boat population) (50%). The highest percentage share of people who believe in side effects of allopathic medicine falls in Dalgate (57%) followed by Manigam (37%), Shallbug (20%), Rainawari (17%), Khonmoh (13%) and Tailbal (10%). The coefficient of correlation between the two variables is –0.67.

SAMPLE VILLAGES IN DISTRICT SRINAGAR

Table 8.1
Correlation between Literacy and Government Employees

S. No	*Name of the Village*	*Literacy Rate*	*% age of Govt. Employee*
1.	Manigam	70	57
2.	Tailbal	33	20
3.	Rainawari	50	30
4.	Dalgate	40	—
5.	Shallbug	63	13
6.	Khonmoh	40	17

Let us show the correlation between literacy rate and Government Employees, using Spearman's rank correlation coefficient method *i.e.*

$$r = 1 - \frac{6\Sigma d^2}{N(N^2 - 1)}$$

Where the letters have their usual meaning.

Solution

Let literacy rate be represented by 'X' and % age of Government employees by 'Y'. RX and RY are the ranks of 'X' and 'Y'.

S. No.	X	Y	RX	RY	d	d^2
1.	70	57	1	1	0	0
2.	33	20	6	3	3	9
3.	50	30	3	2	1	1
4.	40	0	4.5	6	-1.5	2.25
5.	63	13	2	5	-3	9
6.	40	17	4.5	4	0.5	0.25
	N = 6				$\Sigma d^2 = 21.5$	

Using the formula

$$r = 1 - \frac{6\Sigma d^2}{N\left(N^2 - 1\right)}$$

$$= 1 - \frac{6(21.6)}{6(36-1)} = 1 - \frac{129}{210} = \frac{210-129}{120} = \frac{81}{210} = 0.38$$

Since coefficient of correlation is 0.38, hence the correlation between the two variables is positive.

Correlation between Education and Household Hygiene

The following table 8.2 show the literacy rate and household hygiene of six villages of Srinagar (Table 8.2).

Table 8.2

S. No.	Name of the Village	Literacy Rate	% age of Household with unsatisfactory hygiene
1.	Manigam	70	57
2.	Tailbal	33	73
3.	Rainawari	50	33
4.	Dalgate	40	37
5.	Shallbug	63	57
6.	Khonmoh	40	53

Let us show the correlation between literacy rate and unsatisfactory household hygiene using rank difference method *i.e.*

$$r = 1 - \frac{6\Sigma d^2}{N(N^2-1)}$$

Where the letters have their usual meaning.

Solution

Let literacy rate be represented by 'X' and unsatisfactory household hygiene. Government employees by 'Y'. RX and RY are the ranks of 'X' and 'Y'

S. No.	X	Y	RX	RY	d	d^2
1.	70	57	1	2.5	-1.5	2.25
2.	33	73	6	1	5	25
3.	50	33	3	6	-3	9
4.	40	37	4.5	5	-0.5	0.25
5.	63	57	2	2.5	-0.5	0.25
6.	40	53	4.5	4	0	0.25
	N = 6				$\Sigma d^2 = 37$	

Using the formula

$$r = 1 - \frac{6\Sigma d^2}{N(N^2-1)}$$

$$= 1 - \frac{6(37)}{6(36-1)} = 1 - \frac{222}{210} = \frac{210-222}{210} = \frac{-12}{210} = -0.5$$

Since coefficient of correlation is –0.05, hence the correlation between the two variables is negative.

Correlation between Literacy and Use of Traditional Medicine

The following Table 8.3 shows the literacy rate and use of Traditional Medicine in six villages of Srinagar District (Table 8.3).

Table 8.3

S. No.	Name of the Village	Literacy Rate	Use of Traditional Medicine
1.	Manigam	70	0
2.	Tailbal	33	17
3.	Rainawari	50	0
4.	Dalgate	40	0
5.	Shallbug	63	0
6.	Khonmoh	40	13

Let us show the correlation between literacy rate and use of Amchi medicine using rank difference method *i.e.*

$$r = 1 - \frac{6\Sigma d^2}{N(N^2 - 1)}$$

Where the letters have their usual meaning.

Solution

Let literacy rate be represented by 'X' and use of traditional medicine by 'Y' RX and RY are the ranks of 'X' and 'Y'.

S. No.	X	Y	RX	RY	d	d^2
1.	70	0	1	4.5	-3.5	12.25
2.	33	17	6	1	5	25
3.	50	0	3	4.5	-1.5	2.25
4.	40	0	4.5	4.5	0	0
5.	63	0	2	4.5	-.25	6.25
6.	40	13	4.5	2	2.5	6.25
$N = 6$					$\Sigma d^2 = 52$	

Using the formula

$$r = 1 - \frac{6\Sigma d^2}{N(N^2 - 1)}$$

$$= 1 - \frac{6(52)}{6(36-1)} = 1 - \frac{312}{210} = \frac{210 - 312}{210} = \frac{-102}{210} = -0.48$$

Since coefficient of correlation is –0.48, hence the correlation between the two variables is negative.

Correlation between Occupation and use of Unani Medicine

The following table 8.4 provides the data of occupation and use of Unani medicines for six villages of Srinagar (Table 8.4).

Table 8.4

S. No.	Name of the Village	Literacy Rate	% age of Govt. employees
1.	Manigam	30	0
2.	Tailbal	37	17
3.	Rainawari	30	0
4.	Dalgate	20	0
5.	Shallbug	20	0
6.	Khonmoh	50	13

Let us show the correlation between occupation (labour) and use of Unani medicines using rank difference method *i.e.*

$$r = 1 - \frac{6\Sigma d^2}{N\left(N^2 - 1\right)}$$

Where the letters have their usual meaning.

Solution

Let occupation (labour) be represented by 'X' and use of Unani Medicines by 'Y' RX and RY are the ranks of 'X' and 'Y'.

S. No.	X	Y	RX	RY	d	d^2
1.	30	0	3.5	4.5	-1	1
2.	37	17	3	1	1	1
3.	30	0	3.5	4.5	-1	1
4.	20	0	5.5	4.5	1	1
5.	20	0	5.5	4.5	1	1
6.	50	13	1	2	-1	1
	$N = 6$					$\Sigma d^2 = 6$

Using the formula

$$r = 1 - \frac{6\Sigma d^2}{N(N^2 - 1)}$$

$$= 1 - \frac{6(6)}{6(36-1)} = 1 - \frac{36}{210} = \frac{210 - 36}{210} = \frac{174}{210} = -0.82$$

Since coefficient of correlation is 0.82, hence the correlation between the two variables is positive.

Correlation between Literacy rate and Occupation

The following table 8.5 shows the literacy rate and occupation of six villages of Srinagar District (Table 8.5).

Table 8.5

S. No.	*Name of the Village*	*Literacy Rate*	*% age of Govt. employees*
1.	Manigam	70	30
2.	Tailbal	33	37
3.	Rainawari	50	30
4.	Dalgate	40	20
5.	Shallbug	63	20
6.	Khonmoh	40	50

Let us show the correlation between literacy rate and occupation (labour) using rank difference method *i.e.*

$$r = 1 - \frac{6\Sigma d^2}{N(N^2 - 1)}$$

Where the letters have their usual meaning.

Solution

Let literacy rate be represented by 'X' and occupation (labour) 'Y' RX and RY and the ranks of 'X' and 'Y'.

S. No.	X	Y	RX	RY	d	d^2
1.	70	30	1	3.5	-2.5	6.25
2.	33	37	6	2	4	16
3.	50	30	3	3.5	-.5	0.25
4.	40	20	4.5	5.5	-1	1
5.	63	20	2	5.5	-3.5	12.25
6.	40	50	4.5	1	3.5	12.25
N = 6						$\Sigma d^2 = 48$

Using the formula

$$r = 1 - \frac{6\Sigma d^2}{N(N^2-1)}$$

$$= 1 - \frac{6(48)}{6(36-1)} = 1 - \frac{288}{210} = \frac{210-288}{210} = \frac{-78}{210} = -0.37$$

Since coefficient of correlation is –0.37, hence the correlation between the two variables is negative.

Correlation between Income and Occupation

The following table 8.6 shows the income and occupation of six villages of Srinagar District (Table 8.6).

Table 8.6

S. No.	Name of the Village	Literacy Rate	% age of Govt. employees
1.	Manigam	30	30
2.	Tailbal	30	37
3.	Rainawari	23	30
4.	Dalgate	40	20
5.	Shallbug	37	20
6.	Khonmoh	50	50

Let us show the correlation between income and occupation (labour) using rank difference method *i.e.*

$$r = 1 - \frac{6\Sigma d^2}{N(N^2 - 1)}$$

Where the letters have their usual meaning.

Solution

Let income be represented by 'X' and occupation (labour) 'Y', RX and RY are the ranks of 'X' and 'Y'.

S. No.	X	Y	RX	RY	d	d^2
1	30	30	1.5	3.5	1	1
2.	30	37	4.5	2	2.5	6.25
3.	23	30	6	3.5	2.5	6.25
4.	40	20	2	5.5	-3.5	12.25
5.	37	20	3	5.5	-2.5	6.25
6.	50	50	1	1	0	0
$N = 6$						$\Sigma d^2 = 32$

Using the formula

$$r = 1 - \frac{6\Sigma d^2}{N(N^2 - 1)}$$

$$= 1 - \frac{6(32)}{6(36-1)} = 1 - \frac{192}{210} = \frac{210 - 192}{210} = \frac{18}{210} = -0.08$$

Since coefficient of correlation is 0.08, hence the correlation between the two variables is positive.

Correlation between Income and Number of Rooms

The following table 8.7 shows the income and number of rooms of six villages of Srinagar District (Table 8.7).

Table 8.7

S. No.	Name of the Village	% age of households (having income 1600-3000)	Number of Rooms (5-8)
1.	Manigam	30	10
2.	Tailbal	30	30
3.	Rainawari	23	30
4.	Dalgate	40	63
5.	Shallbug	37	17
6.	Khonmoh	50	20

Let us show the correlation between income and number of rooms using rank difference method *i.e.*

$$r = 1 - \frac{6\Sigma d^2}{N\left(N^2 - 1\right)}$$

Where the letters have their usual meaning.

Solution

Let Income be represented by 'X' and number of rooms by 'Y', RX and RY are the ranks of 'X' and 'Y'.

S. No.	X	Y	RX	RY	d	d^2
1.	30	10	4.5	6	-1.5	2.25
2.	30	30	4.5	2.5	2	4
3.	23	30	6	2.5	3.5	12.25
4.	40	63	2	1	1	1
5.	37	17	3	5	-2	4
6.	50	20	1	4	-3	9
	$N = 6$					$\Sigma d^2 = 32.5$

Using the formula

$$r = 1 - \frac{6\Sigma d^2}{N\left(N^2 - 1\right)}$$

$$= 1 - \frac{6(32.5)}{6(36-1)} = 1 - \frac{588}{210} = \frac{210-195}{210} = \frac{15}{210} = 0.07$$

Since coefficient of correlation is 0.07, hence the correlation between the two variables is positive.

Correlation between Income and Toilet Facility

The following table shows the income and toilet facility of six villages of Srinagar District (Table 8.8).

Table 8.8

S. No.	Name of the Village	% age of households (having income 1600-3000)	% age of households having good Toilet Facility
1.	Manigam	30	53
2.	Tailbal	30	30
3.	Rainawari	23	67
4.	Dalgate	40	73
5.	Shallbug	37	27
6.	Khonmoh	50	23

Let us show the correlation between income and toilet facility using rank difference method *i.e.*

$$r = 1 - \frac{6\Sigma d^2}{N(N^2-1)}$$

Where the letters have their usual meaning.

Solution

Let us income be represented by 'X' and toilet facility by 'Y', RX and RY are the ranks of 'X' and 'Y'.

Using the formula

$$r = 1 - \frac{6\Sigma d^2}{N(N^2-1)}$$

S. No.	X	Y	RX	RY	d	d^2
1.	30	53	4.5	3	1.5	2.25
2.	30	30	4.5	4	-5	0.25
3.	23	67	6	2	4	16
4.	40	73	2	1	1	1
5.	37	27	3	5	-2	4
6.	50	23	1	6	-5	25
	$N = 6$				$\Sigma d^2 = 48.25$	

$$= 1 - \frac{6(48.25)}{6(36-1)} = 1 - \frac{285}{210} = \frac{210 - 289.5}{210} = \frac{79.5}{210} = -0.37$$

Since coefficient of correlation is –0.37, hence the correlation between the two variables is negative.

Correlation between Income and Traditional Medicine

The following table 8.9 shows the income and use of traditional medicines of six villages of Srinagar District.

Table 8.9

S. No.	Name of the Village	% age of households (having income 1600-3000)	% age of households using traditional medicines
1.	Manigam	30	0
2.	Tailbal	30	17
3.	Rainawari	23	0
4.	Dalgate	40	0
5.	Shallbug	37	0
6.	Khonmoh	50	13

Let us show the correlation between income and use of traditional medicines, using rank difference method *i.e.*

$$r = 1 - \frac{6\Sigma d^2}{N(N^2 - 1)}$$

Where the letters have their usual meaning.

Solution

Let income be represented by 'X' and use of traditional medicines by 'Y'. RX and RY are the ranks of 'X' and 'Y'.

S. No.	X	Y	RX	RY	d	d^2
1.	30	0	4.5	4.5	0	0
2.	30	17	4.5	1	3.5	12.25
3.	23	0	6	4.5	1.5	2.25
4.	40	0	2	4.5	-2.5	6.25
5.	37	0	3	4.5	-1.5	2.25
6.	50	13	1	2	-1	1
	$N = 6$				$\Sigma d^2 = 24$	

Using the formula

$$r = 1 - \frac{6\Sigma d^2}{N(N^2 - 1)}$$

$$= 1 - \frac{6(24)}{6(36-1)} = 1 - \frac{144}{210} = \frac{210-144}{120} = \frac{66}{210} = 0.31$$

Since coefficient of correlation is 0.31, hence the correlation between the two variables is positive.

Correlation between Use of Allopathic Medicines and Side Effects

The following table 8.10 shows the use of allopathic medicines and side effects of six villages of Srinagar District.

Let us show the correlation between use of allopathic medicines and side effects, using rank difference method *i.e.*

$$r = 1 - \frac{6\Sigma d^2}{N(N^2 - 1)}$$

Table 8.10

S. No.	Name of the Village	Use of Allopathic Medicines	Side Effects
1.	Manigam	63	37
2.	Tailbal	90	10
3.	Rainawari	73	17
4.	Dalgate	50	57
5.	Shallbug	100	20
6.	Khonmoh	63	13

Where the letters have their usual meaning.

Solution

Let use of allopathic medicines be represented by 'X' and side effects by 'Y', RX and RY are the ranks of 'X' and 'Y'.

S. No.	X	Y	RX	RY	d	d^2
1.	63	37	4.5	2	-2.5	6.25
2.	90	10	2	6	4	16
3.	73	17	3	4	1	1
4.	50	57	6	1	-5	25
5.	100	20	1	3	2	4
6.	63	13	4.5	5	0.5	0.25
	$N = 6$					$\Sigma d^2 = 52.50$

Using the formula

$$r = 1 - \frac{6\Sigma d^2}{N(N^2-1)}$$

$$= 1 - \frac{6(52.50)}{6(36-1)} = 1 - \frac{315}{210} = \frac{210-315}{120} = \frac{105}{210} = -0.50$$

Since coefficient of correlation is –0.50, hence the correlation between the two variables is negative.

9

Socio-Cultural, Economic Conditions and Health Care of District Leh: Correlation Analysis

Leh District

Leh town lies at an altitude of 3500 m above sea level. Leh has a permanent population of 35000 inhabitants. There is huge floating population during the short summer season (June-October) when temporary migrant workers and tourists treble the population size. The city is growing uncontrolled and unplanned. The literacy rate is 62.24 per cent.

Table 9.1 shows the literacy rate and its relation with Government employment. The sample villages are Thiksay, Chuchoot, Nemu and Sakti of Leh district. The highest literacy rate is found in Sakti (57%) followed by Chuchoot (46%) and Thiksay (37%). The lowest literacy rate was obtained in Nemu. The highest percentage of Government employees are found in Chuchoot followed by Nemu and Sakti (27% each) and the lowest in Thiksay (23%).

The literacy rate in all four sample villages is higher than the percentage of Government employee. There is the close relation between the two variables in Chuchoot village which is near to the Leh town. This means that the village near the Leh town has highest share in Government employment.

> The co-efficient of correlation between the two variables is 0.35 per cent which indicates the positive correlation. It is obvious that the percentage of Government employment not only depends upon the literacy rate but also on the nearness to the urban centre.

Table 9.2 shows the literacy rate and its relation with household hygiene. The sample villages are Thiksay, Chuchoot, Nemu and Sakti of Leh district. The highest literacy rate is found in Sakti (57%) which has the lowest household hygiene facility. Chuchoot is followed by Sakti with 46 per cent with highest household hygiene facility. Thiksay and Nemu has lowest percentage of literacy rate viz. 37 and 30 per cent with 47 and 33 per cent of household hygiene.

Thus from the above we may conclude that there is no impact of distance factor (from Leh).

> The co-efficient of correlation is –0.13 which shows that there is no interdependence of the two variables.

Table 9.3 reveals the labour work occupation and its relation with usage of *Amchi* medical system. The highest percentage of labour work occupation falls in Sakti (53%) followed by Nemu (37%). The lowest rate of labour work occupation is found in Thiksay and Chuchoot (33% each). The highest usage of Amchi medical system is noted in Thiksay (87%) followed by Nemu and Sakti (33% each) and Chuchoot (73%).

> The co-efficient of correlation between the two variables is 0.1 *i.e.* positive correlation is found between the two. Hence the low income group *i.e.* labour workforce prefer Amchi medical system.

Table 9.4 reveals the relation between literacy rate and labour workforce. The highest literacy rate was found in Sakti (57%) with highest labour workforce (53%) followed by Chuchoot with 46 per cent literacy rate and 33 per cent labour workforce. This is followed by Thiksay with 37% literacy rate and labour workforce with 33 per cent and Nemu with 30 per cent literacy rate and 37 per cent labour workforce.

> The correlation between the two variables is 0.35 which indicates the positive correlation.

Table 9.5 depicts the relation between income range (1600-3000) and labour workforce. The highest percentage of people falling above income range was found in Nemu (50%) with 37 per cent labour workforce. The highest labour workforce was found in Sakti (53%) with 30 per cent population falling in this income range. Thiksay and Chuchoot has 37 and 27 per cent population in this income group with 33 per cent labour workforce.

> The co-efficient of correlation between the two variables is 0.25 which indicates the positive correlation.

Table 9.6 reveals the association between income class (1600-3000) and share of number of rooms (5-8). The lowest percentage of this income was found in Chuchoot *i.e.* 27 per cent with 37 per cent of population having 5-8 rooms. The highest percentage of number of rooms was found in Thiksay (40%) with 37 per cent of household in this income class. The other two villages Nemu and Sakti having 27 and 17 per cent of room share with 50 per cent of household in the above income group.

> The co-efficient of correlation between the two variables is zero which indicates the neutral relationship between the two variables.

Table 9.7 reveals the relationship between income class (1600-3000) and good toilet facilities. The highest share of this income group was found in Nemu (50%) followed by Thiksay (37%), Sakti (30%) and Chuchoot (27%). The highest share of good local facilities was found in Thiksay and Sakti (53%) each followed by Chuchoot (47%) and Nemu (43%).

> The co-efficient of correlation between the two variables is –0.25.

Table 9.8 shows the relation between income class (1600-3000) and usage of Amchi medicines. The highest usage of Amchi medicines was found in Thiksay (87%) with 37% of above this income group, while the lowest usage of Amchi medicines was found in Chuchoot (73%) with lowest percentage of this income group (27%). The other two villages Nemu and Sakti possess 50 and 30 per cent respectively of this income share with 77 per cent usage of Amchi medicines each.

The coefficient of correlation between the two variables is 0.65.

Table 9.9 reveals the association between the side effects of allopathic medicines. The lowest percentage of people avoiding allopathic medicines was found in Thiksay with 3 per cent with highest percentage share of side effects (83%). The other sample villages Chuchoot, Sakti and Nemu avoid allopathic medicines with 27, 23 and 16 per cent respectively. The percentage share of perception of side-effects after Thiksay was highest in Sakti (77%), followed by Nemu and Chuchoot with 73 per cent each.

The coefficient of correlation between the two variables is –0.55.

SAMPLE VILLAGES IN DISTRICT LEH

Correlation between Literacy and Government Employees

The following Table 9.1 shows the literacy rate and number of Government employees (% age) of the four villages of Leh District (Table 9.1).

Table 9.1

S. No.	Name of Village	Literacy Rate	% age of Govt. Employees
1.	Thiksay	37	23
2.	Chuchoot	46	43
3.	Nemu	30	27
4.	Sakti	57	27

In order to compute the correlation between the two variables Spearman's rank correlation coefficient method has been used:

$$r = 1 - \frac{6\Sigma d^2}{N(N^2-1)}$$

Where

r = coefficient of correlation
d = difference between the ranks
N = number of observations

Solution

Let literacy rate be represented by X and % age of Government employees by Y. RX and RY are the ranks of X and Y.

S. No.	X	Y	RX	RY	d	d^2
1.	37	23	3	4	–1	1
2.	47	43	2	1	1	1
3.	30	27	4	2.5	1.5	2.25
4.	57	27	1	2.5	–1.5	2.25
$N = 4$					$\Sigma d^2 = 6.5$	

Using the formula

$$r = 1 - \frac{6\Sigma d^2}{N(N^2-1)}$$

$$= 1 - \frac{6(6.5)}{4(16-1)} = 1 - \frac{39}{60} = \frac{60-39}{60} = \frac{21}{60} = \frac{7}{20} = +0.35$$

Since $r = 0.35$ which is positive hence there is a positive correlation between literacy rate and percentage of Government employees.

Correlation between Education and Household Hygiene

The following table (9.2) provides data of literacy rate and household hygiene of four villages of Leh.

Table 9.2

S. No.	*Name of Village*	*Literacy Rate*	*% of household having unsatisfactory hygiene*
1.	Thiksay	37	47
2.	Chuchoot	46	57
3.	Nemu	30	33
4.	Sakti	57	27

In order to compute the correlation between the two variables rank correlation method has been used:

S. No.	*Name of Village*	*Literacy Rate*	*% of Household using Amchi medicines*
1.	Thiksay	37	87
2.	Chuchoot	46	73
3.	Nemu	30	77
4.	Sakti	57	77

Attempt can also be made to compute the correlation between the two variables using rank correlation method.

$$r = 1 - \frac{6\Sigma d^2}{N(N^2 - 1)}$$

Where

r = coefficient of correlation
d = difference between the ranks
N = number of observations

Solution

Let literacy rate be represented by X and use of Amchi Medicine by Y. Further RX and RY represents the ranks of X and Y.

S. No.	X	Y	RX	RY	d	d^2
1.	37	87	3	1	2	4
2.	46	73	2	4	–2	4
3.	30	77	4	2.5	+1.5	2.25
4.	57	77	1	2.5	–1.5	2.25
	N = 4					$\Sigma d^2 = 12.5$

Using the formula

$$r = 1 - \frac{6\Sigma d^2}{N(N^2 - 1)}$$

$$r = \frac{1 - 6(12.5)}{60} = 1 - \frac{75}{60} = \frac{-15}{60} = \frac{-15}{60} = -0.25$$

Since r –0.3 which is negative, hence there is a negative correlation between literacy and the use of Amchi medicines.

Correlation between Occupation and Amchi Medicines

The following table (9.3) provides data of occupation and use of Amchi medicines.

Table 9.3

S. No.	Name of Village	Literacy Rate	% age of household using Amchi Medicines
1.	Thiksay	33	87
2.	Chuchoot	33	73
3.	Nemu	37	77
4.	Sakti	53	77

In order to study the correlation between the two variables, rank difference method has been used.

$$r = 1 - \frac{6\Sigma d^2}{N(N^2 - 1)}$$

Where letters have their usual meanings. The occupation as labour work be represented by X and use of Amchi medicine as Y. Further RX and RY represent the ranks of X & Y.

Solution

Let literacy rate be presented by X and use of Amchi medicine by Y. Further RX and RY represent the ranks of X and Y.

S. No.	X	Y	RX	RY	d	d^2
1.	33	87	3.5	1	2.5	6.25
2.	33	73	3.5	4	-0.5	0.25
3.	37	77	2	2.5	-0.5	0.25
4.	53	77	1	2.5	-1.5	2.25
N = 4						$\Sigma d^2 = 9.00$

Using the formula

$$r = 1 - \frac{6\Sigma d^2}{N(N^2 - 1)}$$

$$= 1 - \frac{6(9)}{4(16-1)} = 1 - \frac{54}{60} = \frac{60-54}{60} = \frac{6}{60} = +0.1$$

Since $r = +0.1$ is positive, hence there is a positive correlation between the two.

Correlation between Literacy Rate and Occupation

The following table provides data of literacy rate and occupation (Table 9.4).

Table 9.4

S. No.	Name of Village	Literacy Rate	% of Household having Occupation Labour Work
1.	Thiksay	37	33
2.	Chuchoot	46	33
3.	Nemu	30	37
4.	Sakti	57	53

In order to study the correlation between the two variables, rank difference method has been used.

$$r = 1 - \frac{6\Sigma d^2}{N(N^2 - 1)}$$

Where letters have their usual meanings.

Solution

Let literacy rate be represented by X and labour work as Y. Further, RX and RY represent the ranks of X and Y.

S. No.	X	Y	RX	RY	d	d^2
1.	37	33	3	3 5	-0.5	0.25
2.	46	33	2	3 5	-1.5	2.25
3.	30	37	4	2	2	4
4.	47	53	1	1	0	0
	N = 4				$\Sigma d^2 = 6.50$	

Using the formula

$$r = 1 - \frac{6\Sigma d^2}{N(N^2 - 1)}$$

$$= 1 - \frac{6(6.5)}{4(16 - 1)} = 1 - \frac{39}{60} = \frac{60 - 39}{60} = \frac{21}{60} = +0.35$$

Since coefficient of correlation is 0.35 is positive, hence there is positive (+ve) correlation between the two variables.

Correlation between Income and Occupation

The following table provides data of income and occupation (Table 9.5).

Table 9.5

S. No.	Name of Village	% age of Household having income 1600-3000	% age of Household using Occupation Labour Work
1.	Thiksay	33	33
2.	Chuchoot	33	33
3.	Nemu	37	37
4.	Sakti	53	53

In order to study the correlation between the Income and Occupation (labour work) rank difference method had been used, *i.e.*

$$r = 1 - \frac{6\Sigma d^2}{N(N^2 - 1)}$$

Where letters have their usual meanings.

Solution

Let income is represented by 'X' and Occupation by 'Y'. Further 'RX' and 'RY' represent the ranks of 'X' and 'Y'.

S. No.	X	Y	RX	RY	d	d^2
1.	37	33	2	3.5	-1.5	2.25
2.	27	33	4	3.5	0.5	0.25
3.	50	37	1	2	-1	1
4.	30	53	3	1	2	4
	N = 4					$\Sigma d^2 = 7.50$

Using the formula

$$r = 1 - \frac{6\Sigma d^2}{N(N^2 - 1)}$$

$$= 1 - \frac{6(7.5)}{4(16-1)} = 1 - \frac{45}{60} = \frac{60-45}{60} = \frac{15}{60} = +0.25$$

Since coefficient of correlation is 0.25, which is positive, hence there is positive (+ve) correlation between the two variables.

Correlation between Income and Number of Rooms

The following table provides data of Income and Number of Rooms (Table 9.6).

Table 9.6

S. No.	*Name of Village*	*% age of Household having Income 1600-300*	*% age of Household using Number of Rooms (5-8)*
1.	Thiksay	37	40
2.	Chuchoot	27	37
3.	Nemu	50	27
4.	Sakti	30	17

In order to study the correlation between the Income and Number of Rooms, rank difference method has been used, *i.e.*

$$r = 1 - \frac{6\Sigma d^2}{N(N^2 - 1)}$$

Where letters have their usual meanings.

Solution

Let income be represented by 'X' and Number of Rooms by 'Y'. Further 'RX' and 'RY' represent the ranks of 'X' and 'Y'.

S. No.	*X*	*Y*	*RX*	*RY*	*d*	d^2
1.	37	40	2	1	1	1
2.	27	37	4	2	2	4
3.	50	27	1	3	-2	4
4.	30	17	3	4	-1	1
	$N = 4$					$\Sigma d^2 = 10$

Using the formula

$$r = 1 - \frac{6\Sigma d^2}{N(N^2 - 1)}$$

$$= 1 - \frac{6(10)}{4(16-1)} = 1 - \frac{60}{60} = \frac{60-60}{60} = \frac{0}{60} = 0$$

Since coefficient of correlation is 0, hence there is not any correlation between Income and Number of Rooms.

Correlation between Income and Toilet Facility

The following table provides data of Income and Toilet Facility (Table 9.7).

Table 9.7

S. No.	*Name of Village*	*% age of Household having Income 1600-3000*	*% age of Household using Toilet Facility*
1.	Thiksay	37	53
2.	Chuchoot	27	47
3.	Nemu	50	43
4.	Sakti	30	53

In order to study the correlation between the Income and Toilet Facility, following rank difference method has been used, *i.e.*

$$r = 1 - \frac{6\Sigma d^2}{N(N^2 - 1)}$$

Where letters have their usual meanings.

Solution

Let income is represented by 'X' and Toilet Facility by 'Y'. Further 'RX' and 'RY' represent the ranks of 'X' and 'Y'.

S. No.	X	Y	RX	RY	d	d^2
1.	37	53	2	1.5	0.5	0.25
2.	27	47	4	3	1	1.0
3.	50	43	1	4	–3	9.0
4.	30	53	3	1.5	1.5	2.25
	N = 4					$\Sigma d^2 = 12.50$

Using the formula

$$r = 1 - \frac{6\Sigma d^2}{N(N^2 - 1)}$$

$$= 1 - \frac{6(12.5)}{4(16-1)} = 1 - \frac{75}{60} = \frac{60-75}{60} = \frac{-15}{60} = -0.25$$

Since coefficient of correlation is –0.25, which is negative, hence there is negative (–ve) correlation between the two variables.

Correlation between Income and use of Amchi Medicine

The following table provides data of Income and use of Amchi medicines of four villages of Leh (Table 9.8).

Table 9.8

S. No.	Name of Village	% age of Household having Income 1600-3000	% age of Household using Toilet Facility
1.	Thiksay	37	87
2.	Chuchoot	27	73
3.	Nemu	60	77
4.	Sakti	30	77

In order to study the correlation between the Income and use of Amchi medicines, using rank difference method has been used, *i.e.*

$$r = 1 - \frac{6\Sigma d^2}{N(N^2 - 1)}$$

Where letters have their usual meanings.

Solution

Let income be represented by 'X' and use of Amchi medicines by 'Y'. Further 'RX' and 'RY' represent the ranks of 'X' and 'Y'.

S. No.	X	Y	RX	RY	d	d^2
1.	37	87	2	1	1	1
2.	27	73	4	4	0	0
3.	50	77	1	2.5	-1.5	2.25
4.	30	77	3	2.5	0.5	0.25
$N = 4$					$\Sigma d^2 = 3.50$	

Using the formula

$$r = 1 - \frac{6\Sigma d^2}{N(N^2-1)}$$

$$= 1 - \frac{6(3.5)}{4(16-1)} = 1 - \frac{21}{60} = \frac{60-21}{60} = \frac{-39}{60} = +0.65$$

Since coefficient of correlation is +0.65, which is positive, hence there exists positive (+ve) correlation between the two variables.

Correlation between use of Allopathic Medicines and Side Effects

The following table provides data of use of Allopathic medicines and Side effects (Table 9.9).

Table 9.9

S. No.	Name of Village	% age of Household not using Allopathic Medicines	% age of Household with perception of Side Effects
1.	Thiksay	03	83
2.	Chuchoot	27	73
3.	Nemu	16	73
4.	Sakti	23	77

In order to study the correlation between Allopathic medicines and Side effects, rank difference method has been used, *i.e.*

$$r = 1 - \frac{6\Sigma d^2}{N(N^2 - 1)}$$

Where letters have their usual meanings.

Solution

Let Allopathic medicines be represented by 'X' and Side effects by 'Y'. Further 'RX' and 'RY' represent the ranks of 'X' and 'Y'.

S. No.	X	Y	RX	RY	d	d^2
1.	03	83	4	1	3	9
2.	27	73	1	3.5	–2.5	6.25
3.	16	73	3	3.5	–0.5	0.25
4.	23	77	2	2	0	0
	$N = 4$					$\Sigma d^2 = 15.50$

Using the formula

$$r = 1 - \frac{6\Sigma d^2}{N(N^2 - 1)}$$

$$= 1 - \frac{6(15.50)}{4(16 - 1)} = 1 - \frac{93}{60} = \frac{60 - 93}{60} = \frac{-33}{60} = -0.55$$

Since coefficient of correlation is –0.55, which is negative, hence there is no correlation between the two variables.

10

Health Care Behaviour in Kashmir

John Gold (1980) has defined behavioural geography as a branch of geography that adopts the behaviouralist approach to man-environment relationship, where explanation of spatial patterns of behaviour is sought primarily in cognitive processes that underpinned that behaviour. Cognition is defined as the mental processes by means of which people acquire, organize, and use knowledge.

Hippocrates, who lived in the fifth century B.C., was probably the first scholar who laid emphasis on the study of health behaviour in his famous treatise "On Airs, Waters and Places". The emphasis in Hippocrates' work was not only on the impact of the environment upon the health of the people, but also the mode in which the inhabitants live and what are their pursuits, whether they are fond of drinking and eating to excess, and given to indolence, or are fond of exercise and labour, and not given to excess in eating and drinking (Adams 1849, 190-191).

In geography, behavioural perspective was incorporated in studies by Julian Wolpert, an American geographer at Princeton. Wolpert's monumental work on the decision process in spatial perspective examines farmers' behaviour in Central Sweden, has direct relevance to the geography of health care behaviour (Wolpert 1964). He compared spatial variations in agricultural practice with the pattern of variation in labour productivity. The model shown in Figure 10.1 may provide a link from a general perspective of man-environment relationship to one of health and health seeking behaviour.

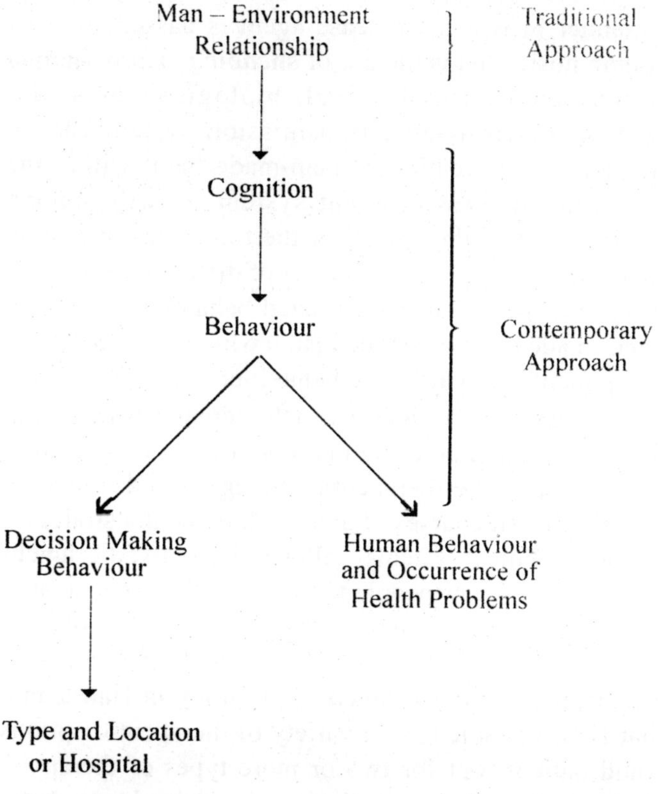

Figure 10.1: Model: Geography of Health Behaviour

From a spatial standpoint, it is relatively easy to describe the ways in which human behaviour may affect the communicable disease hazard. Specific agents cause communicable diseases. The agents are living organisms, each with their own obligatory cycle of survival. These life cycles may include associations with humans, other living organisms, or specific types of physical environments. Furthermore, any part of the agent life cycle may be associated with specific time constraints. Thus, human behaviour affects disease transmission in four ways (Roundy 1987). First human behaviour may alter the likelihood of a new human host becoming parasitized with the disease agent. This is the act of exposure. Second, human behaviour may control the place and manner in which a disease agent is passed from an infected human host. This is the act of shedding. Third, human behaviour may create the physical, biological, or social environment in which disease transmission system can be successful. This is the creation of man-made habit within the parameters of the successful agent system. Fourth, human behaviour may result in the spread of the transmission system from one place to another. This is the act of diffusion. Thus, the identification of a specific disease related behaviour-exposure, shedding, man-made habitats and diffusion which occur in space, are vital components of health care behaviour.

Health seeking behaviour focuses on the actual ways in which people conceptualize and perceive matters of illness and health, how they decide upon the therapeutic strategies, and how they implement their chosen courses of action. Therapeutic strategies pertain to various medical systems—allopathic, ayurvedic, amchi and unani systems, and how people from various socio-economic strata opt for a particular system. Type of illness also plays a significant role in choosing a medical system. Robert Stock, a Canadian medical geographer, noted in his study in Hausaland, Nigeria, that Hausa people have a variety of therapeutic options available, and patients opt for two or more types of therapy—herbal remedy, modern pharmaceuticals and an Islamic prophetic medicine, concurrently (Stock, 1987).

Surinder M. Bhardwaj, a geographer based at Kent State University, USA in a study carried out in rural areas of Punjab, concludes that exclusive patronage of indigenous medicine and its practitioners is very limited and that people either prefer allopathic medicine or opt for a variety of available treatments. He suggests that expectancy of cure rather than the system of medicine seems implicit in the preference of a medical system (Bhardwaj, 1975).

Indian Context

Today traditional medicine co-exist with complements, and competes against scientific medicine throughout most of the developing world (Good, 1977). Similarly in Kashmir the unani medical system co-exist with allopathic medical system. In a notable study on medical pluralism Bhardwaj pointed out that unani medical system dominates in Kashmir (Bhardwaj, 1980).

The present policy of Government of India, both at the Centre and States is to encourage the traditional system of medicine in different parts of India irrespective of their cultural linkages of communities with a particular medical system.

In the last several years the Central Council for Research in Unani Medicine, New Delhi has achieved significant leads in the research programmes. At present there are twenty-two institutions under the council which are functioning in different parts of the country including Regional Research Institute of Unani Medicine, Srinagar, Kashmir.

The popularity of unani system of medicine may be analysed by the fact that in 1984 there was one unani drug shop in Hazratbal locality in Srinagar town. Today more than fifty unani private shops are found in and around Hazratbal locality of Srinagar. In addition to this, according to a report, published from Regional Research Institute of Unani Medicine of Srinagar in 1992, states that the response of patients in OPD, of that Institute has increased to such an extent that the concerned physicians are compelled to overstay in the OPD and despite the disturbed conditions in the State the patients seeking treatment is increasing overwhelmingly during the last few years.

Examples from Kashmir: (Dard and Gurez Valley)

Distribution and Socio-Economic Characteristics of Traditional Practitioners

There are four unani practitioners, one in each Bagtor, Dawar, Tallel and Baduab villages besides the religious persons practising spiritual medical system one each in Korgbal, Kanzalwan,

Manzgund, Sardab and Gujran villages. Social characteristics of traditional practitioners show some interesting features. All of them were male within the age of 50-68 years, illiterate, with no formal training but have learned the art of healing from their parents. Unani practitioners were prescribing medicines prepared out of the raw material collected from local materia medica, free of cost but were paid small amount after recovery. All of them were found practising at their own houses as an additional work (Akhtar and Rather, 1999).

Utilization of Medical System

Analysis of data reveals that traditional medical system was utilized by majority (70.00%) of households in the sample villages. Utilization of allopathic medical system was noted only in 17.50 per cent of sample households and the shift from one medical system to another was noted only among 12.50 per cent of total households surveyed (Table 10.1). Utilization of traditional medical system was hundred per cent in each of the sample villages of Baduab, Badugam and Tallel, however the utilization of same medical system 50 per cent in the village Dawar and 52 per cent in the village Kanzalwan. Allopathic medical system was utilized only by 32 per cent of sample in the village Kanzalwan and 20 per cent

Table 10.1: Utilization of Medical System by Sample Villages

Sample Village	No. of households surveyed	*Medical system utilized by households in %*					
		Allopathic		*Unani*		*More than one*	
		No. of households	*%*	*No. of households*	*%*	*No. of households*	*%*
Dawar	30	6	20.00	18	60.00	6	20.00
Kanzalwan	25	8	32.00	13	52.00	4	16.00
Tallel	10	—	—	10	100.00	—	—
Badugam	05	—	—	5	100.00	—	—
Baduab	10	—	—	10	100.00	—	—
Total	80	14	17.50	56	70.00	10	12.50

Source: Field work.

of households in the village Dawar. Surprisingly the utilization of allopathic medical system was not noted in the village of Badugam, Baduals and Tellel. Shift from traditional allopathic and vice-versa was noted among a small percentage (20%) in the village Dawar and 16 per cent in the village Kanzalwan.

Perception of Disease

The study of people's perception of disease reveals the level of understanding about a disease. It is evident from the table (Table 10.2) that about 32.50 per cent of the patients surveyed considered the cause of the disease due to supernatural forces and did not take any medicine. They believed that a curse of God caused disease and thus pray to Almighty for recovery. Perception of disease due to magic was noted in 22.50 per cent whereas perception of disease due to bad luck was noted among 17.50 per cent of total patients surveyed. Perception of disease due to change in food and perception of disease due to bad air was noted in 16.55 and 11.25 per cent of patients respectively. A considerable variation in different types of perception of disease has been identified in the sample village (Table 10.2)

Management of Health Problems

Inter-regional differences within the valley show different types of management of health problems (Table 10.3). Analysis of the table shows that largest percentage of households surveyed (26.67) do not report to the hospital or any other type of health practitioner for a couple of days but practised home remedies. About 16.39 per cent of the households were found discussing the health problem within the family and 12.22 per cent discussed health problems with the friends. A large group of households (24.72%) consulted unani practitioner for various health problems. Allopathic medical facilities were attended by only 12.50 per cent of the households and 10 per cent purchased medicines directly from the medical shop in advance for various health problems. Variation in different types of management for different types of ailments is shown in the Table 10.3.

Table 10.2: Perception of Disease by Sample Villages

Sample Village	No. of Pats. Interviewed	Perception of disease (% to total)									
		Disease due to nature		Disease due to bad luck		Disease due to magic		Disease due to change in food		Disease due to bad air	
		Cases	%	Cases	%	Cases	%	Cases	%	Cases	%
Kanzalwan	20	6	30.00	4	20.00	3	15.00	5	25.00	2	10.00
Dawar	26	8	30.77	4	15.38	3	11.54	5	19.23	6	23.08
Tallel	14	4	28.57	2	14.33	5	35.71	2	14.23	1	7.14
Badugam	12	4	33.34	2	16.67	5	41.66	1	8.33	—	—
Baduab	08	4	50.00	2	25.00	2	25.00	—	—	—	—
Total	80	26	32.50	14	17.50	18	22.50	13	16.25	9	11.25

Source: Field work.

Table 10.3: Management of the Health Problems

Health Problems	*No. of house-holds surveyed*	*Discuss in the family for home remedies*											
		No. of house holds	*% to total*	*Discuss with friends*		*Purchased from shops*		*Consult traditional practitioner*		*Go to hospital*		*Do not go for few days*	
Fever/Typhoid	80	18	22.50	8	10.00	6	7.50	12	15.00	12	15.00	2	30.00
Cough/Cold	80	10	12.50	6	07.50	4	5.00	08	10.00	06	7.50	46	57.50
Anaemia	80	2	2.50	14	17.50	6	7.50	20	25.00	08	10.00	20	25.00
Diarrhoea	80	8	10.00	20	25.00	6	7.50	24	30.00	16	18.18	6	7.50
Eye Disease	80	6	7.50	8	10.00	10	12.50	30	37.50	10	12.00	16	18.18
TB/Asthma	80	12	15.00	6	7.50	4	5.00	20	25.00	08	9.09	30	37.50
Stomach Pain	30	14	17.50	8	9.09	8	10.00	16	18.18	20	25.00	14	17.50
Fracture	80	20	25.00	8	10.00	4	55.00	28	25.00	06	7.50	14	17.50
Others	80	18	22.50	10	12.50	6	7.50	20	25.00	04	5.00	22	27.50
Total	720	118	16.23	88	12.22	54	7.50	178	24.72	90	12.50	192	26.67

Source: Field work.

Traditional medical system is dominant over allopathic as it is socially, culturally and environmentally close to the people that is, it is their own health care system and is accepted, practised and utilized by them. It also has a potential for wider utilization at a low cost as it uses the local materia medica and its development in such tribal area would give due respect to the people's culture and heritage.

Srinagar City and Hinterland

The study aims at describing the patient's utilization pattern of out-patient (OPD) of Regional Research Institute of Unani Medicine in Srinagar.[1] Demographic, socio-economic and medical data were collected through questionnaire and personal interviews by the author from a 20 per cent sample (n. 100) of patients in the year 1995 and 1996. Interview was conducted during the summer months of June and July. Practitioners working in the institute were also interviewed covering various aspects of their healing system (Table 10.4).

Table 10.4: Reasons that Patients Reported for Seeking Medical Care

Sample patients suffering from various diseases/illnesses	
Diseases/Illnesses	*Per cent*
Arthritis	22
Vitiligo	21
Kidney problem	13
Liver disorder	10
Bronchoid Asthma	10
Others	24

1. Regional Research Institute of Unani Medicine, Srinagar was established in 1986, attracting large number of patients belonging to Srinagar city as well as from distant places/districts. The efforts of the research workers of the Institute resulted in bringing out the achievement of the unani medicine on the forefront. The institute made some achievements in Waj-ul-asfasil (Rheumatoid Arthritis) Bars (Vitiligo) Zae-Qun-Nafs (Bronchoid Asthma) and Deedan-e-Ama (Helminthiasis).

Findings

In reported cases, 54 per cent were adult females, 30 per cent were adult males and 16 per cent were children upto 12 years of age. Clinic's clientele belong to different places even from far off districts/cities.

Almost 68 per cent of patients were patronising the clinic after going through the modern medical system. Twenty per cent came directly and twelve per cent after using other traditional medical system such as homoeopathy and ayurveda. In some cases patients were turning towards unani medical system after using modern medical system for several years. The main complaint expressed by these patients was that drugs prescribed under allopathic treatment provided only temporary relief, and have subsequent side effects. Ninety two per cent of patients were suffering from arthritis and 64 per cent suffering from vitiligo came via hospital or after using modern medical system. Most patients suffering from urinary problems, headache, depression, kidney problem came to the unani clinic after using modern medical system.

During the interview arthritis and vitiligo were found the most commonly reported problems. In addition to these, kidney problem, liver disorder and bronchoid asthma together constitute more then 75 per cent of the total reported disease/illness, noted during the interview (Table 10.4).

Patients belonging to Srinagar city as well as distant places were using the Unani Clinic for the treatment of various problems. An analysis of utilization pattern of the Unani Clinic shows that the pattern of utilization changes as the distance increases from the clinic. Clientele residing in nearby localities *i.e.*, within a kilometre from the clinic come even for minor complications such as cough and cold (due to seasonal change), stomach upset, pimples etc. Contrary to that patients coming from distant places/ districts were using the Unani Clinic only for serious chronic problems. Some cases are referred to the Clinic even from prestigious SMSH Hospital, as well as cities of Lucknow, Delhi and Bombay. In distant places most cases are reported for vitiligo, bronchoi asthma, arthritis, skin disorder, peptic ulcer etc. Patients from Banihal, Lolab sometimes come for 2/3 days to pay visits to clinic.

In an interview, practitioners of the Unani Clinic claimed that physicians started giving their references for some chronic diseases and some of them prescribe medicine which were earlier prescribed by these practitioners of unani medicine such as Liver B.

It is interesting to mention that in some previous studies it was found that unani medicine was appropriate for adults than children because more patience is required and the longer time necessary for unani therapy to take effect. Parents have a tendency to seek the more immediate relief available at modern clinics for young children, particularly for infectious diseases, which constitute the majority of pediatric complaints (Nachinda, 1977; Izhar, 1990). Contrary to these previous analysis, the practitioners of this Unani Clinic claimed that parents are becoming more and more aware about the side-effects of medicine prescribed under allopathic treatment, and now they are using this traditional unani system for the treatment of their children in several cases.

Doru Tehsil

In another study conducted in Doru Tehsil (Tak, 2001), the findings show that people perceive various diseases differently in different villages. The study covers 10 villages as sample out of 79 villages. The sample villages constitute 12.65 per cent of total villages of the Doru Tehsil. From each sample village, 30 households were randomly surveyed and the health information from each head of the family was collected. The surveyed households including their family heads perceive poor water supply, bad housing, lack of health facilities, bad weather conditions and transport problems as health hazards. Moreover, the people perceive health problems related to income, education, age and occupation of the head of the households. A brief description is given below:

Perception of Health Problems in Sample Villages

Table 10.5 reveals the perception of various health problems like poor water supply, poor transport, lack of health facilities and bad housing in sample villages of Doru Tehsil. One of the health problems like contaminated water is highest in Hakura (25%) followed by Vessu (23%), Kriri (22%), Hengipora (20%), Mundah (19%), Larkipora (19%), Qammar (18%), Rakhi Lissar (16%), Batagund (15%) and Verinag (10%). Another health problems perceived in Doru Tehsil is the poor transport facilities.

The highest transport problem is in Rakhi Lissar (20%) followed by Hengipora (19%), Batagund (15%), Mundah (13%), Qammar (12%), Hakura (11%), Verinag (7%), Kriri (5%), Larkipora (3%) and Vessu (2%).

One more health problem perceived in the study area is the lack of health facilities. Lack of health facilities in sample villages has been noted significantly in Rakhi Lissar (93.3%), followed by Hengipora (83.3%), Qammar (73.3%), Larkipora (73.3%), Mundah (70%), Vessu (70%), Batagund (66.6%), Kriri (66.6%), Verignag (63.3%) and Hakura (63.3%).

Bad housing is the most important health hazard perceived in the study area and in Hengipora nearly 96.6 per cent of the population perceive bad housing as most important health hazard followed by Rakhi Lissar (90%), Qammar (83.3%), Batagund (63.3%), Mundah (60%), Kriri (50%), Larkipora (46.6%), Hakura (40%) and Vessu (36.6%).

Health Care Behaviour

The health behaviour of people in Daru Tehsil is governed by the rugged topography of the area.

The study shows that rough terrain and undeveloped means of transport has greatly influenced the people's health care behaviour. The health centres in Doru Tehsil are unevenly distributed. At higher elevation their number declines. The rural areas have been largely neglected. The poor accessibility of health centres greatly restricts the movement of sick people who are deprived of medical

Table 10.5: Perception of Health Problems

Sample Village	*No. of household surveyed*	*Perception of health problems by household in %*							
		Poor water supply		*Poor transport*		*Lack of health facility*		*Bad housing*	
		No. of H.H.	*Per cent*	*No. of H.H.*	*Per cent*	*No. of H.H.*	*Per cent*	*No. of H.H.*	*Per cent*
Hengipora	30	20	66.6	19	63.3	25	83.3	29	96.6
Qammar	30	18	60	12	40	22	73.3	25	83.3
Batagund	30	15	50	15	50	20	66.6	19	63.3
Verinag	30	19	63.3	7	23.3	19	63.3	16	53.3
Mundah	30	19	63.3	13	43.3	1	70.0	18	60.0
Kriri	30	22	73.3	5	16.6	20	66.6	15	50.0
Rakhi Lissar	30	16	53.3	20	66.6	28	93.3	27	90.0
Larkipora	30	19	63.3	3	10	22	73.3	14	46.6
Hakura	30	25	83.3	11	36.6	19	63.3	12	40.00
Vessu	30	23	76.6	2	6.6	21	70.0	11	36.6

Source: Field Survey by M.A. Tak.

Note: H.H. = Households.

treatment. In the study area people are not generally aware about the cause of ill health and the availability of health facility. Majority of people of Doru Tehsil are illiterate and follow traditional way of life. These problems have led to different types of behaviour of people towards different diseases. It has been observed that in villages where health facilities are not available within the easy reach of people the response to health problems is quite different to those having accessibility to good health facilities. People hardly pay a second visit to the doctor in villages located far off from health facilities.

Most of the people practice self-medication and buy medicines from the shop without consulting any doctor. The people do not take allopathic medicines due to their being expensive or having the opinion of their side effects on health. They also believe in treatment of Hakims for several diseases. It has been observed that they do not discuss the diseases and their treatment like diarrhoea with their friends, however for diseases like TB, most of the people discuss it with their friends about their treatment as they consider it a serious health problem.

In most of the villages traditional medical practitioners available are not professionally trained and most of them suggest same type of treatment for different diseases. Table 10.6 reveals the health care behaviour of patients towards various types of treatment *e.g.* for some diseases they discuss with friends, for some diseases they were inclined towards allopathic treatment and for some they used unani or any other traditional treatment.

Table 10.7 reveals that health care behaviour varies during winter months as well. Most people in case of influenza and cold as well as in case of fever buy medicines from the shop. Similarly variation occur in the utilization of allopathic system of medicines as well as traditional medical system. For example in Hengipora some 30 per cent use allopathic medicines in case of influenza and cold, while traditional treatment is accepted by 60 per cent of the population. In village Kriri about 90 per cent population utilize allopathic medicines in case of respiratory diseases and asthma and only 5 per cent go for traditional treatment.

Table 10.6: Health Care Behaviour of Patients in Summer

	Buy medicine from shop (self-medication)				*Discuss with friends*				*Allopathic Treatment*				*Traditional treatment*			
	I	*II*	*III*	*IV*	*I*	*II*	*III*	*IV*	*I*	*II*	*III*	*IV*	*I*	*II*	*III*	*IV*
Hengipora	6	20	25	15	—	—	5	10	40	30	30	25	54	50	40	50
Qammar	15	10	20	10	—	—	10	10	35	30	30	50	50	55	40	30
Batagund	10	15	25	50	5	10	25	5	15	30	10	35	70	45	40	10
Verinag	50	5	70	90	5	5	5	—	20	5	15	5	25	85	10	5
Mundah	10	20	60	50	10	10	—	15	5	10	10	25	75	60	25	25
Kriri	30	10	10	35	10	10	—	15	25	15	45	30	35	65	45	20
Rakhi Lissar	15	10	20	10	—	—	—	—	50	45	60	45	35	45	20	45
Larkipora	40	25	60	70	10	15	—	5	10	20	20	10	40	40	20	1
Hakura	10	5	70	5	—	25	—	10	30	60	20	45	60	10	10	40
Vessu	20	60	70	35	—	20	5	—	60	10	5	55	20	10	20	10

Source: Field Survey by M.A. Tak

Note: Diarrhoea = I, Dysentery = II, Vomiting = III, Eye diseases = IV.

Table 10.7: Health Care Behaviour of Patients in Winter

	Buy medicine from shop (self medication)				Discuss with friends				Allopathic treatment				Traditional treatment			
	I	*II*	*III*	*IV*	*I*	*II*	*III*	*IV*	*I*	*II*	*III*	*IV*	*I*	*II*	*III*	*IV*
Hengipora	10	5	10	20	—	20	—	—	30	30	50	40	60	55	40	50
Qammar	15	20	10	20	5	10	—	—	40	40	50	40	40	30	40	40
Batagund	25	10	5	20	—	5	—	—	50	65	70	70	25	20	25	10
Verinag	40	10	5	50	—	2	—	—	55	58	75	40	5	30	20	10
Mundah	15	20	10	20	5	10	—	—	40	40	50	40	40	30	40	40
Kriri	50	5	20	45	—	—	—	—	45	90	75	45	5	5	5	10
Rakhi Lissar	10	5	10	20	—	2	—	—	30	30	50	40	60	55	40	40
Larkipora	45	20	10	60	—	—	—	—	45	75	88	35	10	5	10	5
Hakura	45	20	10	60	—	—	—	—	45	75	80	35	10	5	10	5
Vessu	40	10	5	20	—	5	—	—	50	65	70	70	10	20	25	10

Source: Field Survey by M. A. Tak

Note: Diarrhoea = I, Dysentery = II, Vomiting = III, Eye diseases = IV.

In India, where most people both in rural and urban areas are very poor, and unhygienic conditions lead to such circumstances, contact with parasitic disease agents is constant and unavoidable. Researchers need to understand the relationship between behaviour and disease transmission. There is a need to understand the web of relationships among factors such as water, sanitation, agricultural practices, rural development and health in different geographical regions. Research must also focus upon the pattern of health seeking behaviour of people of different socio-economic strata in different regions including their perception of disease and the type of medical care accepted by them. Such studies may contribute significantly in health care planning in developing countries such as India.

REFERENCES

Adams, F. (1849). *The Genuine Works of Hippocrates* London: The Sydenham Society.

Akhtar, R. and Rather, G.M. (1999). Health care behaviour in Dards: A case study of Gurez valley, *Jour Central Asian Studies,* 10, No. 1, 121-42.

Akhtar, R. and Learmonth, A.T.A. (1977). The resurgence of malaria in India-1965-1976. *GeoJournal* 1:5, 69-80.

Beals, A.R. (1976). Strategies of resort to curers in South India, in C. Leslie (editor), *Asian Medical System: A Comparative Study,* Berkeley, University of California Press, 184-200.

Bhardwaj, Surinder M. (1975). Attitudes towards different systems of medicine: A survey of four villages in Punjab, *Social Science and Medicine* 9:603-12.

Gold, J.R. (1980). *An Introduction to Behavioural Geography.* New York: Oxford University Press.

Good, C.M. (1977). Traditional medicine: An agenda for medical geography, *Social Science and Medicine,* 11: 705-713.

Hunter, John M. (1966). River blindness in Nangodi, Northern Ghana: A hypothesis of cyclical advance and retreat, *Geographical Review,* 56, 398-414.

Hunter, John M. (1997). Geographical patterns of guineaworm infestation in Ghana. An historical contribution, *Social Science and Medicine* 44: 1: 103-22.

Hyma, B. and Attur, Ramesh (1980). The reappearance of malaria in Sathanur reservoir and environs, Tamil Nadu, *Social Science and Medicine* 1733-44.

Izhar, Nilofar (1990). Patient origins and usage of a Unani Clinic in Aligarh town, India. *Social Science and Medicine* 30, 10:1139-41.

Izhar, Nilofar (1994). Health care behaviour in rural areas of Kulgam tehsil, Anantnag, Kashmir Himalayas, *Geographia Medica* 432-44.

Kloos, H. *et al.* (1983). Water contact behaviour and schistosomiasis in an Upper Egyptian village, *Social Science and Medicine* 17, 545-62.

Nchinda, T.C. (1977). A household study of illness prevalence and health care preferences: Rural district of Cameroon, *International Journal of Epidemiology, 6:* 235-241.

Prothero, R.M. (1977). Disease and mobility: A neglected factor in epidemiology, *International Journal of Epidemiology* 6:3:69-80.

Regional Research Institute of Unani Medicine (1992) *Report on Activities and Achievements*, Srinagar.

Roundy, R. (1987). Human behaviour and disease hazards in Ethiopia. In Rais Akhtar (ed). *Health and Disease in Tropical Africa,* London, Harwood Academic Publishers, 261-76.

Stock, R. (1987). Understanding health care behaviour: A model together with evidence from Nigeria. In Rais Akhtar (ed.). *Health and Disease in Tropical Africa.* London: Harwood Academic Publishers, 279-92.

Tak, M.A. (2001). *Health Seeking Behaviour of the Rural Areas of Doru Tehsil,* Unpublished M. Phil dissertation. Department of Geography, University of Kashmir, Srinagar.

Watts, S. *et al.* (1998) The study of human behaviour and schistosomiasis transmission in an irrigated area. *Social Science and Medicine* 46:6. 755-65

Wolpert, Julian (1964). The decision process in spatial perspective. *Annals of the Association of American Geographers* 54, 537-58.

11

Planning Perspective

In the context of health care planning of the three physically and socio-economic and culturally distinct districts–Srinagar, Jammu and Leh, planners must take into account the following:

1. Equity Criterion

There should be equity in the distribution of health care facilities. The present concentration of health care facilities in the region should be balanced as much as possible by the placement of facilities in undeserved areas. Although it is impossible to assess the health care needs consequent decision about the location of health care facility must cover maximum population of the area.

2. Need-Based Planning

Priority should be given to villages/communities most in need. Prioritization is important because it ensures that scare resources are first spent on more needy villages/communities and that a greater proportion of the available resources are allocated to such villages/communities. The assessment of the needs must identify the type of health care facilities *i.e.*, Amchi and Unani in Leh, Ayurveda in Jammu, and Unani in Srinagar, as well as allopathic, based on the people's attitude and behaviour towards disease and health care facility; which should receive priority above others.

3. The Population Size of the Region

The population size is an important indicator and its spatial pattern must be kept in all planning perspectives.

4. The Perception of People using Public Health Services

No data exists on the perception of the population using public/private health services, and the type of medical system being used by the population. Research must be conducted to ascertain the utilization of health services and medical systems. What per cent of population is being served by the health care facility, and the percentage variation in different travelling distance zones *i.e.* 5 kms, 10 kms, 15 kms, 20 kms and above? We must also take into account the physiographic barriers which hamper accessibility to health care facility. Such investigation will be useful in identification of gaps in the provision of health care facility, which can be focused for future development of facilities.

The two factors which we feel are responsible for this urban bias are the type of medical education, and the role of the Government. The pattern of medical education is one which is a replica of the developed countries resulting in a demand for the 'latest' and the 'best' in medical care. The result is an urban biased, hospital-oriented, curative-care model with focus on chronic/lifestyle disease.

The Government has also enhanced the urban bias by investing heavily in urban-centered health facilities, often at the expense of the larger rural population.

After having spent several years in the medical college in urban areas, even a doctor coming from the rural areas would not want to go back to serve his/her own rural villages. Lack of infrastructural development in the rural areas particularly, hospital/health centre building and poor network, lack of good educational facilities for children present another model that discourages doctors to serve in rural areas. To make health services available to the rural remote mountainous areas of Jammu and Kashmir, on a more equitable pattern it would require a greater investment in rural infrastructure in general and in rural health care facilities in particular. Market based financing, particularly in large urban centres, created more unequal access to health care between the rich and the poor. It would also require a restructuring of the medical curriculum, such as the scheme of Medical Assistance, practiced in some East African countries, to suit the needs of the local population *i.e.*, treatment, control and eradication of communicable infectious, and waterborne diseases. It is true that by coercing doctors by passing laws making it mandatory to serve rural areas, and by building a few rural health centres, will not serve the purpose until the process of overall development touches the vast and inaccessible mountainous areas of Jammu and Kashmir.

Nonetheless, the scenario of people's health status is determined by a myriad of factors; economic well-being, education, diet, lifestyle and health care. In the health care domain, the contribution to better health status come principally from public health measures, prevention, basic primary care services and the availability of essential life saving drugs. It has been experimented in China that a nation does not need sophisticated educated health personnel to deliver basic health care. The experience illustrated that as mentioned earlier about the practice of employing the Medical Assistant in East African countries, health workers with six months to one year of training after matric school could competently perform preventive and basic services, with focus on infectious disease, malaria (in Jammu), waterborne diseases (in Srinagar) and respiratory, skin diseases (in Leh). Lastly, since the allopathic medical system is expensive, it is need of the hour to encourage indigenous systems of medicine, *i.e.*, Ayurveda (Jammu) Unani (Srinagar) and Amchi (Leh).

5. Village Level Health Posts

With reference to accessibility, the example of Vietnam is relevant. In Vietnam, under outreach programme, village-level health posts are being established, together with a hamlet based "collaborator" network. Locally selected collaborators are provided with bicycles to ensure that links can be made between settlements and the nearest health post when health care is needed. In most remote and inaccessible areas, especially in Ladakh region, establishment of such village health posts will go a long way in taking health care to door step of Ladakhi people. Non-availability of health personnel to serve remote and inaccessible areas, is an important constraint in the delivery of health care. Establishment of mobile health services and training of regional medical and nursing personnel helps to solve regional personnel shortages and meet demand for medical services in remote areas in general, and mountainous districts of Ladakh and Kashmir regions in particular. Access to health services is a particular problem for women especially in remote mountainous areas. Special efforts need to be made to reach them. For reducing the functional gaps, locational planning has to be adopted in two phases. These are short-term plan and long-term plan. In both phases, health care facilities are provided in two ways:

1. Through the population threshold, and
2. Through some central villages.

Locational Analysis

Bryan Massam and R. Azuma (1983) in their paper entitled. "Rural policy-making and the location of public facilities: Problems and a method", present one possible approach to the village location problem using a hypothetical example for a rural region shown on Figure 11.1.

The problem posed here is to evaluate the set of 20 villages and determined the best group of three for the location of dispensary. The criteria used for evaluation include:

(a) Average distance travelled (a measure of private costs, in terms of time and money),
(b) Standard deviation of distances (a measure of equity),
(c) Maximum distance (a measure of equity),
(d) Per cent population served by the nearest village (a measure of effectiveness),
(e) Construction costs (a measure of public costs),
(f) Per cent population within 10 kms of a village (a measure of effectiveness), and

(g) Per cent population within 25 kms of village (a measure of effectiveness).

The evaluation matrix is shown in Table 11.1. This matrix is analysed using concordance analysis and multi-dimension scaling. Full details are provided in Massam (1975). A summary of the results for this hypothetical problem are provided below.

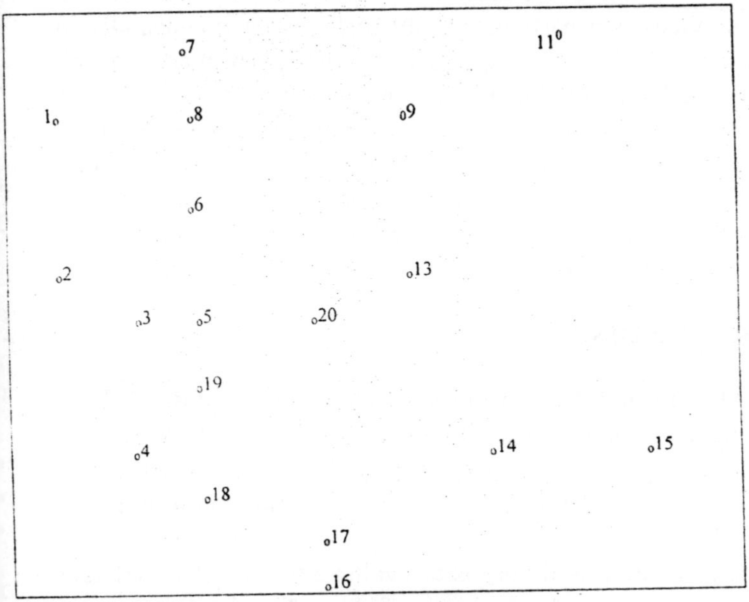

Figure 11.1

Potential Sites for Facility Location

Village	*Population*	*Village*	*Population*	*Village*	*Population*
01.	1500	08.	5500	15.	1400
02.	3000	09.	25000	16.	3000
03.	5000	10.	4500	17.	2000
04.	3200	11.	9000	18.	2100
05.	6000	12.	6000	19.	2400
06.	3300	13.	4000	20.	3100

Note: This figure has been modified by the author taking into Account realities in rural India.

A set of 5 villages (5, 9, 17, 3, 20) were selected from the set of 20. From this small group 10 combinations of three villages were identified. They are shown below as the ten strategies.

Strategies	*Villages (See Figure 1)*		
01.	5	9	17
02.	5	3	17
03.	5	20	17
04.	3	9	17
05.	3	20	17
06.	20	9	17
07.	5	20	9
08.	3	20	9
09.	5	3	9
10.	5	3	20

A series of experiments were conducted under different weighting schemes for the criteria. From these experiments it appeared that strategy 4 or 1 is the best. This suggests that services should be located at 9 and 17. The third village could be either 5 or 3, both are equally attractive.

In summary we suggest that the problem of selecting villages to receive public services is important in national and regional planning. Attempts to tackle this problem using distance-minimizing location criterion, albeit an important one. In an attempt to overcome this weakness a multi-criteria framework is developed. A test of this approach is offered using a hypothetical problem.

In holistic healthcare planning, the measurement of levels of health is vital, and the required indices can be divided in the following three groups:

(a) Those associated with the health status of population in given area (vital statistics, nutrition, immunization);
(b) Those related to physical and socio-economic and cultural conditions having more or less direct bearing on the health status of the areas under review; and
(c) Those concerned with health services and activities directed towards the improvement of health conditions (availability and use of hospitals, physicians and other personnel).

Table 11.1: Basic Impact Matrix

	Policies				Best				Worst			
	1	2	3	4	5	6	7	8	9	10	11	12
1. Average distance d (km)	7.4	10.6	10.6	10.2	12.9	11.8	12.0	15.0	11.9	14.5	7.4	15.0
2. Standard deviation σ (km)	8.4	13.5	12.1	7.0	10.3	7.5	11.8	9.7	12.0	13.9	7.0	13.9
3. Maximum distance max (d) (km)	35.4	57.0	50.3	28.3	50.3	35.4	35.4	30.8	30.4	50.3	28,3	57.0
4. % of population served by the nearest site (%)	80.6	75.5	69.6	49.8	40.4	51.7	60.0	37.1	66.0	55.0	80.6	37.1
5. Construction cost (Y 10000C)	1379	1489	13516	1144	1063	1085	1331	1039	1424	1337	1039	1489
6. % of population within 15 km to facility (%)	90.9	74.6	76.2	82.6	77.7	79.6	63.2	59.7	61.4	50.5	90.9	50.5
7. % of population within 25 kr to facility (%)	96.1	82.3	82.4	96.1	84.2	94.5	86.7	80.7	79.5	66.8	96.1	66.8

Planning Perspective must take into account the following:

1. The scope of the types of health services and of the population covered by any particular plan must be comprehensive in character.
2. The health plan must take into account the concrete demographic, social, cultural, economic, and administrative conditions existing in the concerned region.
3. In all stages of the development and implementation of a health plan, the conscientious observation, recording and evaluation of the fu!fillment of the plan are necessary.

REFERENCE

1. Massam, B. H. and Azuma, R. (1983). Rural policy-making and the location of public facilities: Problems and a method. *Human Geography*, Geographic Institute, Kyoto University, Japan, pp. 80-89. Also see Massam, B.H. (1975) *Location and Space in Social Administration*, London, Edward Arnold. Also see, Massam B. H., Akhtar, R. and Askew, I (1986) Applying operating research to health planning: Locating health centers in Zambia, *Health Policy and Planning*. Vol. 1, No. 4, pp. 326-334; Massam, B.H. (1990) Location-Allocation Models in health care planning. In R. Akhtar (ed.) *Environment and Health: Themes in Medical Geography*. A.P.H; New Delhi, pp. 153-168.

Appendix

Block Srinagar Tehsil Srinagar

Distance (kms) from Village upto............

Name of the Village	Dispensary				Family Planning Centre				Child Health Centre			
	1981	1994-95	1996-97	2000-01	1981	1994-95	1996-97	2000-01	1981	1994-95	1996-97	2000-01
Ahal	2	3	3		7	7	7		20	7	7	
Bad-Uder	2.5	2	2		12.5	12	12		9	12	12	
Burzhama	0	0	0		7	5	5		18	5	5	
Baghi-Lalpandit	2	3	3		12	10	10		12	10	10	
Balhama	4	0	0		4	10	10		14	10	10	
Bakshipora (Tangamarg)	0	1	1		11	11	16		9	11	7	
Chattir-hama	0	0	0		7	7	7		20	7	7	
Dara	4	0	0		4	25	25		28	40	40	
Faqir-Gujri	6	30	30		6	45	45		30	45	45	
Guripora	[illegible].5	1	1		1.5	15	15		8	15	15	
Gtaundi Rehman	5	3	3		6	6	6		25	6	6	
Gadura	[illegible]	3	1		6	6	6		25	6	6	
Gassu	[illegible]	1	1		6	4	4		17	4	4	
Gagarzoo	3	3	3		13	9	8		9	9	8	
Haran	5	3	0		6	6	6		25	6	6	
Khonmoh	3	0	0		14	8	8		14	8	8	
Krishbal	2	4	4		10,5	4	4		12	4	4	
Khimber	1	1	1		7	8	8		22	8	5	
Muftibagh	3	8	8		25	40	40		25	30	30	
Nurinderbagh	3.5	8			24	30			24	30		
Palpora	0	0	0		7	3	9		10	3	9	
Saidpora (Bala)	3	3			3	30			25	30		
Shunglipora	[illegible].5	3	3		9	9	8		10.5	9	8	

(*Contd.*)

Name of the Village	Dispensary				Family Planning Centre				Child Health Centre			
	1981	1994-95	1996-97	2000-01	1981	1994-95	1996-97	2000-01	1981	1994-95	1996-97	2000-01
Sampora	1	N			14	N			14	N		
Sangam	4	5	5		14	6	6		14	6	6	
Rakhi-waripora	5	3	1		6	6	6		25	6	6	
Takya- Sangrishi	5	0	8		5	16	4		16	16	14	
Wani Hama	6	8	1		12	14	4		27	14	4	
Tanctechama (Inderhama)	[illegible]	0	1		6	6	4		17	17	4	
Zawrah	3	2	2		14	13	13		14	14	13	
Zewan	0	0	0		14	6	5		14	6	6	
Miaguad	5	0			18	18			18	18		
Lawipora	5	2	2		12	19	19		12	19	19	
Malroo	1	1.5	2		5	16	26		5	16	7	
Gundi-Hassi-Bhat	6	3	3		13	20	20		13	20	20	
Achenamble	4.5	2	2		14	10	10		14	10	10	
Zainakoot	—	N			—	N				N		
Shalteng	—	N			—	N				N		
Danihama	2	3	3		2	21	21		21	19	5	
Faqir-Mulnar (Mulnar)												
Bakshipora (Ghat)	0	1			10	R			12			
Saidpora Achan	4	R			7	R			9	R		
Qamarwari Ghat	—	N			—	N				N	—	
Parimpora Ghat	2	N			3	N			5.5	N		
Sliatteng Ghat	2	N			8	N			8	N		
Malroo Ghat	3	N			9	N			9	N		
Mujgund Ghat	0	N			12	N			12	N		
Anehar (Dagpora)	2	N			13	N			13	N		
Dedmari Bagh	—	—	1		—	—	8		—	—	8	
Batpora	N	0	0		N	17	15		N	17	0	

Block Kangan Tehsil Kangan

Distance (kms) from Village upto..........

Name of the Village	Dispensary				Family Planning Centre				Child Health Centre			
	1981	1994-95	1996-97	2000-01	1961	1994-95	1996-97	2000-01	1981	1994-95	1996-97	2000-01
Nilgrar	01	0	1		14	27	23		67	27	23	
Sonamarg	0	0	0		13	25	22		66	25	22	
Porajat Gariangair	01	0	0		6	14	16		59	14	16	
Kullen	0	0	0		4	12	15		58	12	15	
Ravel	01	2	2		2	10	14		56	10	14	
Gund Sarsing	0	0	0		0	9	13		62	9	13	
Fraw Haknar	2	2	1		2	8	12		53	8	12	
Sumbalbala	4	5	5		6	7	12		59	7	11	
Soraf Raw	1.5	1	15		18	8	12		58	8	11	
Hari Ganwan	0	0	12		16	8	12		56	8	12	
Thune	2.5	2	2		10	7	7		50	7	7	
Manuner	1	0	0		13	9	9		53	9	9	
Dard-Uder	3	2	2		7	7	8		47	7	8	
Hayan Palpora	2	6	3		7	6	6		47	6	6	
Aechhama	1	2	3		6	6	7		46	6	7	
Cheerwan	0	0	5		8	6	5		48	6	5	
Sathrina	0	2	4		4	2	4		44	2	4	
Margund	2	1	1		2	1	1		42	1	1	
Kangan	0	0	0		0	0	0		40	0	0	
Hardupanzan	1	1	1		1	1	1		41	1	1	
Kijpora	1.5	1	1		1.5	1	1		39	1	1	
Balmlina	1.5	3	2		1.5	3	3		41.5	3	3	
Bema Bugh	2.5	4	0		2.5	4	5		42.5	4	5	
Khanan	5.5	0	2		5.5	5	6		45.5	5	6	
Wangath	0	0	0		12	10	10		52	10	10	

(*Contd.*)

Name of the Village	Dispensary				Family Planning Centre				Child Health Centre			
	1981	1994-95	1996-97	2000-01	1961	1994-95	1996-97	2000-01	1981	1994-95	1996-97	2000-01
Gund Aril	4	2	6		4	2	6		40	2	6	
Larie	4	2	3		4	2	3		38	2	3	
Drugtanga	4	2	4		6	2	4		39	2	4	
Katch Nambal	0	2	5		3	2	5		40	2	5	
Bar Wallah	0	1	2		2	1	2		39	2	2	
Plang	3	2	3		3	2	3		37	1	3	
Arie Gorie Pora	3	1	3		4	2	5		36	2	5	
Chather	0	0	0		7	5	8		37	2	8	
Chinar	1.5	8	1		4.5	8	5		38.5	8	5	
Ussan	0	7	0		6	7	6		34	7	6	
Najwannallah	1	2	2		2	2	2		42	2	2	
Tanghi Chather	1	1	1		2	1	1		42	1	1	
Akhal	0	1	1		1.5	1	1		41.5	1	1	

Block Lar Tehsil Kangan

Distance (kms) from Village upto.........

Name of the Village	Dispensary				Family Planning Centre				Child Health Centre			
	1981	1994-95	1996-97	2000-01	1981	1994-95	1996-97	2000-01	1981	1994-95	1996-97	2000-01
Haripora	2	2	2		6	2	2		32	8	8	
Arhama	0	3	3		7	3	3		33	10	10	
Anderwan	1	5	5		8	5	5		34	12	12	
Manigam	0	0	0		8	7	7		32	7	7	
Wata Lar	0	1.5	1		9	9	9		34	6	0	
Baghi Mahamand	1	2	2		9.5	2	2		34.5	2	2	
Baghizaman Gania	0.5	3	3		2	2	2		33.5	3	3	
Benihama	1	3	3		3	3	3		35.5	1.8	1.8	
Chunthan Gulanpora	1.5	1.5	1		2	2	2		34.5	3.5	3.8	
Chuntwaliwar	5	4.5	4		5	5	5		38	3.5	3.8	
Qasba-Lar	0	0	0		0	0	0		33	0.5	0.5	
Repora	0.5	0.5	0		0.5	0.5	0		33.5	3	2	
Barsoo	3	0	0		3	3	3		33	5	5	
Wandhama	2	1	1		0.2	2	2		32	5	5	
Khranihama	1	0.5	0		1	1	1		36	3	2	
Kurhama	0	0	0		5	5	5		35	5	5	
Yangora	6	2	2		7	7	7		36	7	7	
Lariwaza	6	6	6		8	8	8		36	9	9	
Tehroo	3	3	3		4	4	3		25	3	3	
Dangerpora	2	1	1		4	2	3		27	3	3	
Bardalla	2	0	0		4	4	4		27	4	4	
Watal Bagh	2	2	2		4	4	4		27	6	6	
Wahid-Pora	3	3	3		3	3	5		24	4	4	
Waskura	1	1	1		1	1	1		39	0	0	
Ahan	2	1	1		1	1	1		38	7	7	

(*Contd.*)

Name of the Village	Dispensary				Family Planning Centre				Child Health Centre			
	1981	1994-95	1996-97	2000-01	1981	1994-95	1996-97	2000-01	1981	1994-95	1996-97	2000-01
Kharbagh	1	2	2		4	4	4		39	8	8	
Zazna	3	2	2		5	5	5		37	7	7	
Badampora	4	2			6	6			37	8		
Zarigund	2	2	2		3	3	3		39	7	7	
Batiwena	0	0	0		4	4	4		36	8	8	
Korag-Domarg	1.5	1	1		1.5	1	1		37	1	1	
Rakh-Rabitar	1	1	1		14	1	1		34	1	1	
Shickh Zoo	2	2	1		9	9	5		28	5	6	
Khanpora	2	2	2		4	4	4		40	8	8	
Gozahama	1	3	3		4	4	4		37	7	7	
Nawabagh	2	2	1		4	9	4		37	7	7	
Daab	1	1	1		1	1	1		40	1	1	
Baghi-Dab												
Rabitar-Gund Roshan	2	0	0		2	1.5	1		4	1.5	1	
Narayanbagh	0	0	0		15		1		41	0	1	
Batipora Dab	1.5	4			4	4			40	9		
Wakura	0	0	1		0	0	1		36	0	0	
Kokagund	1	1	1		3	1	1		33	1	1	
Gamwara	0.5	1	1		13.3	1	1		32	1	1	
Rabitar Gund Roshan (Ghat)	1	1.5			14	1.5			36	1.5		

Block Ganderbal Tehsil Ganderbal

Distance (kms) from Village upto.........

Name of the Village	Dispensary				Family Planning Centre				Child Health Centre			
	1981	1994-95	1996-97	2000-01	1981	1994-95	1996-97	2000-01	1981	1994-95	1996-97	2000-01
Tulmullah	0	0	0		0	0	0		28	28	28	
Sehpora	0	0	0.5		9	7	3		27	27	24	
Chandina Deh (Nowabad)	0	0	0		0	6	6		30	31	31	
Devpora	0.5	3	3		10	7	9		28	28	28	
Gugigund	3	2	2		3	8	8		27	30	30	
Kostorepora	7	3	3		7	9	9		29	29	29	
Gundimoomin	3	3	3		7	5	5		29	29	29	
Hakimgund	4	5	5		8	5	5		30	30	30	
Hotbareh	1.5	5	5		8	6	6		30	30	30	
Saloorah	1	0	0		1	10	1		24.5	25	25	
Shallabug	1	0	0		9	9	9		31	29	29	
Kuijar	3	2	2		4	4	4		26	26	26	
Malapora	2	0.5	0		1.5	3	3		22.5	23	23	
Shahpora	2	0.5	0.5		2	3.5	3		24	24	24	
Budderkund	2	1	1		2	3.5	3		24	24	24	
Bandaybagh	2.5	3	2		2.5	3	3		24.5	28	27	
Nunnar	0	0	6		5.5	6	6		27	27	27	
Badusipora	1	2	2		6.5	7	7		28	28	28	
Sarich-Chowdri Bagh	2	2	2		3	3	3		25	29	29	
Sadar Bagh	2	2			6	3			27.5	29		
Arich	2	0	0		2.5	6	6		24	28	28	
Wayil	0	0	0		9	8	8		31	28	28	

(Contd.)

Name of the Village	Dispensary				Family Planning Centre				Child Health Centre			
	1981	1994-95	1996-97	2000-01	1981	1994-95	1996-97	2000-01	1981	1994-95	1996-97	2000-01
Chaper Gund	0.5	0.5	0.5		5.5	7	7		27	29	29	
Gotli Bagh	0	0	0		13	10	10		35	33	33	
Urpash	2	1	1		8	7	7		28.5	29	29	
Khalamullah	3	3	1		4	7			16	16		
Busser Bugh	1	1.5	1.5		5	6	6		16	16	16	
Baba Daryadin	9	8	8		10	10	10		24	19	19	
Rangil	3	4	4		4	6	6		18	14	14	
Nagbal	3	4	4		3	4	4		19	14	14	
Darand	3	2	2		3	5	5		19	14	14	
Malla Shahi Bagh	2	3	3		2	4	4		21	16	16	
Shuhama	0	0	0		4	6	6		12	18	18	
Warpoh	0.5	0.5	0		3	8	8		13	13	13	
Boqra	2	0.5	0.5		4	7	7		14	10	10	
Hadorah	3	1	1		3	14	14		13	11	11	
Wanihama	3	5	5		3	14	14		12	11	11	
Saidpora Hamchi	0	0	0		3	7	7		13	18	18	
Hordo Muradabad	1	2	2		3	5	5		25	27	27	
Rakh Kujar	—											
Tulmullah Ghat Forest Block	0	N			4	N			26	N		

Block Srinagar Tehsil Srinagar

Percentage Difference of Distance (in kms) to Nearest Health Service Facility (1981-1994, 95)

Name of the Village	Dispensary		Family Planning Centre		Child Health Centre	
	% age Decrease	% age Increase	% age Decrease	% age Increase	% age Decrease	% age Increase
Ahal	—	33.3	0	0	65	—
Badi-Uder	20	—	4	—	—	33.3
Burzhama	0	0	28.5	—	72.2	—
Baghi-Lalpandit		33.3	16.6	—	16.6	—
Balhama	100		—	60	28.5	—
Bakshipora (Tangamarg)		100	0	0	—	18.1
Chattirhama	0	0	0	0	65	—
Dara	100		—	84	—	30
Faqir-Gujri		80	—	66.6	—	33.3
Guripora	33.3	—	—	90	—	46.6
Gundi Rehman	40	—	0	0	76	—
Gadura		100	0	0	76	—
Gassu	0	0	33.3	—	76.4	—
Gagarzoo	0	0	30.7	—	0	0
Haran	40	—	0	0	76	—
Khanmoh	100	—	42.8	—	42.8	—
Krishbal		50	61.9	—	66.6	—
Khimber	0	0	—	12.5	63.6	—
Muftibagh		62.5	—	37.5	—	16.6
Nurinder Bagh		56.2	—	20	—	20
Palpora	0	0	57.1	—	70	—
Saidpora (Bala)	0	0	—	90	—	16.6
Shunglipora		50	0	0	4.7	—
Sampora	N	N	N	N	N	N
Sangam		20	57.1	—	57.1	—

(Contd.)

Name of the Village	Dispensary		Family Planning Centre		Child Health Centre	
	% age Decrease	% age Increase	% age Decrease	% age Increase	% age Decrease	% age Increase
Rakhi-Waripora	40	—	0	0	76	—
Taken Waripora	100	—	—	68.7	0	0
Takya-Sangrishi		25	—	14.2	66.6	—
Wani Hama		100	42.8	—	77.7	—
Tandechama (Inderhama)	100	—	0	0	0	0
Zawrah	50	—	7.1	—	0	0
Mujgund	100	—	0	0	0	0
Lawipora	60	—	—	36.8	—	36.8
Malroo		33.3	—	68.7	—	68.7
Gundi-Hassi-Bhat	50	—	—	35	—	35
Achenamble	55.5	—	28.5	—	28.5	—
Zainakoot	N	N	N	N	N	N
Shalteng	N	N	N	N	N	N
Danihama		33.3	—	90	73.6	—
Faqir Mulnar (Mulnar)		—	—	—	—	—
Bakshipora (Ghat)		100	N	N	N	N
Saidpora Achan	N	N	N	N	N	N
Qamarwari Ghat	N	N	N	N	N	N
Panmpora Ghat	N	N	N	N	N	N
Shalteng Ghat	N	N	N	N	N	N
Malroo Ghat	N	N	N	N	N	N
Mujgund Ghat	N	N	N	N	N	N
Anchar (Dagpora)	N	N	N	N	N	N
Dedmari Bagh	N	N	N	N	N	N
Zewan	0	0	57.1		57.1	
Batpora						

Block Lar Tehsil Kangan

Percentage Difference of Distance (in kms) to Nearest Health Service Facility (1981-1994 and 1995)

Name of the Village	Dispensary		Family Planning Centre		Child Health Centre		Distance to (Kms) (2001)			
	% age Decrease	% age Increase	%age Decrease	%age Increase	%age Decrease	%age Increase	Hospital	Dispensary	FPC	CHC
Haripora	0	0	66.6		75		6	0	2	8
Archama		100	57.1		69.6		8	3	3	10
Anderwan		80	37.5		64.7		10	4	5	12
Manigam	0	0	25		78.1		6	0	7	7
Wat lar		100	0	0	82.3		8	2	2	2
Baghi Mahamand		50	78.9		94.2					
Baghizaman Gania		83.3	0	0	94.9		9	3	2	0
Benihama		66.6	0	0	89.8		8	2	3	2
Chunthan Gulanpora	0	0	0	0	90.7					
Chuntwaliwar	10		0	0	98.4		9	1	5	4
Qasba-Lar	0	0	0	0	91		6	0	0	0
Repora	0	0	0	0	84.8		6	0.5	0.5	0
Barsoo	100		0	0	84.3		7	0	3	3
Wandhama	50			90	91.6		7	0	4.5	3
Khranihania	50		0	0	85.7		8	0	6	6
Kurhama	0	0	0	0	80.5					
Yangora	66.6		0	0	75		8	0	6	0
Latiwaza	0	0	0	0	88		8	0	6	2
Tehroo	0	0	0	0	88.8					
Dangerpora	50		50		85.1		4	3	3	4
Bardalla	100		0	0	77.7		4.5	0	4	0
Watal Bagh	0	0	0	0	83.3		4	0	5	0
Wahid-Pora	0	0	0	0	100		1.5	0	4	0

(*Contd.*)

Name of the Village	Dispensary		Family Planning Centre		Child Health Centre		Hospital	Dispensary	FPC	CHC
	% age Decrease	% age Increase	%age Decrease	%age Increase	%age Decrease	%age Increase	2001	2001	2001	2001
Waskura	0	0	0	0	81.5					
Ahan	50		0	0	94.4		7.0	0	2	2
Kharbagh		50	0	0	81					
Zazna	33.3		0	0	78,3		8.0	0	0	0
Badampora	50		0	0	82					
Zarigund	0	0	0	0	77.7		7	0	4.2	2
Batiwena	0	0	0	0	97.2					
Korag-Domarg	33.3		33.3'		97.2					
Rakh- Rabitar	0	0	92.8		97					
Shiekh Zoo	0	0	0	0	82.1					
Khanpora	0	0	0	0	80					
Gozahama		66.6	0	0	81					
Nawabagh	0	0	0	0	81					
Daab	0	0	0	0	97.5					
Baghi-Dab										
Rabitar-Gund Roshan	100			100	62.5					
Narayanbagh	0	0		100	100					
Batipora Dab		62.5	0	0	77.5					
Wakura	0	0	0	0	100					
Kokagund	0	0		66.6	96.9					
Gamwara		50		92.5	96.8					
Rabitar Gund Roshan (Ghat)	50		89.2		95.8					

Block Ganderbal Tehsil Ganderbal

Percentage Difference of Distance (in kms) to Nearest Health Service Facility (1981-1994 and 95)

Name of the Village	Dispensary		Family Planning Centre		Child Health Centre		
	% age Decrease	% age Increase	% age Decrease	% age Increase	% age Decrease	% age Increase	
Tulmullah	0	0	0	0	0	0	0
Sehpora	0	0	22.2	—	—	0	0
Chandina Deh (Nowabad)	0	0	—	100	100	—	3.2
Devpora	—	83.3	30	—	—	0	0
Gugigund	33.3	—	—	62.5	62.5	—	10
Kostore pora	57.1	—	—	22.2	22.2	0	0
Gundi moomin	0	0	28.5	—	—	0	0
Hakimgund	—	20	37.5	—	—	0	0
Hotbareh	—	70	25	—	—	0	0
Saloorah	100	—	—	90	90	—	2
Shallabug	100	—	0	0	0	—	6.4
Kujjar	33.3	—	0	0	0	—	—
Malapora	75	—	—	50	50	—	2.1
Shahpora	75	—	—	42.8	42.8	0	0
Budder kund	50	—	—	42.8	42.8	0	0
Banday bagh	—	16.6	—	16.6	16.6	—	12.5
Nunnar	0	0	—	8.3	8.3	0	0
Badusipora	—	50	—	7.6	7.6	0	0
Sarich-Chowdri Bagh	0	0	0	0	0	—	13.7
Sadar Bagh	0	0	50	—	—	—	5.1
Arich	100	—	—	58.3	58.3	—	14.2
Wayil	0	0	11.1	—	—	3.2	—
Chaper Gund	0	0	—	21.4	21.4	—	6.8
Gotii Bagh	0	0	23	—	—	5.7	—

(*Contd.*)

(Contd.)

Name of the Village	Dispensary		Family Planning Centre		Child Health Centre		
	% age Decrease	% age Increase	% age Decrease	% age Increase	% age Decrease	% age Increase	
Urpash	50	—	87.5	—	—	—	1.7
Khalamullah	0	0	—	42.8	42.8	0	0
Busser Bugh	—	33.3	—	16.6	16.6	0	0
Baba Daryadin	11.1	—	0	0	0	20	—
Rangil	—	25	—	33.3	33.3	22.2	—
Nagbal	—	25	—	25	25	26.3	—
Darand	33.3	—	—	40	40	23.8	—
Malla Shahi Bagh	—	33.3	—	33.3	33.3	—	22.2
Shuhama	0	0	—	33.3	33.3	—	—
Warpoh	0	0	—	62.5	62.5	0	0
Boqra	75	—	—	42.8	42.8	28.5	—
Hadorah	66.6	—	—	78.5	78.5	15.3	—
Wanihama	—	40	—	78.5	78.5	8.3	—
Saidpora Hamchi	0	0	—	57.1	57.1	—	27.1
Hordo Muradabad	—	50	—	40	40	—	7.4
Rakh Kujar	—	—	—	—	—	—	—
Tulmullah Ghat	—	—	—	—	—	—	—
Forest Block	—	—	—	—	—	—	—

Index